# Becoming Agile

# Becoming Agile

## Coaching Behavioural Change
## for Business Results

*Laura Re Turner*

 Open University Press

Open University Press
McGraw-Hill Education
8th Floor, 338 Euston Road
London
England
NW1 3BH

email: enquiries@openup.co.uk
world wide web: www.openup.co.uk

and Two Penn Plaza, New York, NY 10121-2289, USA

First edition published 2021

A catalogue record of this book is available from the British Library

ISBN-13: 9780335249039
ISBN-10: 0335249035
eISBN: 9780335249046

Library of Congress Cataloging-in-Publication Data
CIP data applied for

Typeset by Transforma Pvt. Ltd., Chennai, India

# Praise for Becoming Agile

*"This book is perfect for business leaders, entrepreneurs, and indeed anyone new to the world of agile leadership. Re Turner engages brilliantly with recent scholarship and thinking, as well as with the real-world situations we all face."*

—David Taylor, Founder, Naked Leader

*"In today's hectic life Agility has become more important than ever and the question is not only "What is it?" but even more "How do I get there?". Acquiring Agility requires deep disruptive change and so deeper understanding, understanding the needs, seeing the value and therefore making it a part of you is essential. It is a coach's responsibility to help people, teams and organisations in that journey. Read this book and cherry pick what helps you out. Enjoy!"*

—Arie van Bennekum, Co-author of the Agile Manifesto,
www.arievanbennekum.com

*"The worlds of agile project management and coaching have evolved largely separately — yet each has much to learn from the other. Here we have a pragmatic and readily applicable approach to integrating both concept and practice across these two evolving domains".*

—David Clutterbuck, Special Ambassador,
European Mentoring and Coaching Council

*"This book is a great resource for coaches who want to continue developing skills that will support leaders, teams, and organizations in building business agility. Laura creatively explores the connection of individuals to the whole through the Six Lenses of Systemic Team Coaching, weaves in both theory and practice, and grounds herself in the agile mindset, leaving flexibility for professional coaches to decide how they will apply this learning. This book is an important read for all professional coaches."*

—Ahmed Sidky, Ph.D., President of the International
Consortium for Agile (ICAgile)

Praise for Becoming Agile

# Contents

# Preface

*'Everyone deserves an opportunity to be heard.'*

This is the statement I wrote on a whiteboard at Henley Greenlands when asked by our tutor, Alison Hardingham, to write a personal statement of what we believe as a coach. It turns out that not only does everyone deserve an opportunity to be heard, but businesses benefit greatly when people at all levels are heard. And more often lately, I find myself advising leaders to give their tough problems to the team to solve. Agile frameworks have promoted self-organizing teams for decades, and the creators of them have learned from leadership and management practices, teamwork and collaboration, and systems thinking.

This is the book I have been wanting to write since starting my MSc in Coaching and Behavioural Change in 2015, when I made the connection that the working style espoused in Agile frameworks is the same as the recommendations for great leadership in organizations. As organizations' use of Agile frameworks has matured, Agile Coaches' toolkits have matured to include professional coaching and working with systems; at the same time, businesses have had to acknowledge the increasing complexity of their organizations – often the complexity is of their own creation – and complexity in the business environments in which they operate. Our business leaders and the coaches who work with them are making the connection that Agile frameworks address the challenge of getting new products to market in highly competitive and uncertain environments, and the way to survive is to develop people who can adapt, instead of introducing new processes and tools.

Having the joy drained from work was the reason I became a coach. It wasn't clear at the time but it's clear in hindsight. My coach training started with a certificate programme at Henley Business School, which led to their MSc in Coaching and Behavioural Change. I felt lucky to be able to write my dissertation, which included small-scale but original research, on success factors for Agile teams. And then I was excited to be able to do that in a coaching context. It was also around this time that I understood I needed to write a book that linked Agile principles and behaviours with the guidance on leadership and effective teams that we've known for decades. As you'll read in my interview with Lyssa Adkins, co-founder of the Agile Coaching Institute (with Michael Spayd) and author of *Coaching Agile Teams*, I believe the world of work was ready for this full-scale assault on command-and-control management that drains the life out of people, and Agile is the branding that is driving the change forward.

As I progressed through my coach training at Henley Business School, I became aware of links among what I knew as success factors for agile organizations, good leadership, and coaching. I consider the following table a work in progress that will evolve, at least in my mind, as I continue working at the intersection of agile behaviours and coaching. How would you add to it, from your own experience? You might use the case studies throughout the book to add to your own table of example behaviours.

| Agile mindset | Leadership | Coaching |
| --- | --- | --- |
| Reflection at intervals (aka Retrospectives) | Self-care | Reflection-in-action |
| Running experiments | One-to-ones | Reflective writing Supervision |
| Outcome-based planning Setting Sprint Goals | Strategic thinking | Goal-setting (by coachee) |

My first hope for this book is to increase the amount of professional Agile Coaching. And that by doing this, organizations will experience sustainable change on their journey to becoming agile. I also hope that buyers of Agile Coaches will respond in kind by reframing their idea of Agile Coaches as people who empower and play the long game of change, instead of doing the work for others by setting up tools and prescribing processes.

A colleague from my coaching supervision group remarked lightly that this book is a 'Covid baby'. That is, it was written during the first UK lockdowns in spring and summer 2020. I was contracted anyway to write the book, and its birth during that time was coincidence rather than deliberate. Nevertheless, the period heightened awareness for many of us the connection between our individual actions and our impact on the whole of society. For example, wearing masks – an act of compassion to protect others – has a positive impact on our hospitals and the economy. Other large-scale impacts of our individual behaviour are not so easy to notice. For example, our choices about what clothes to buy, food to buy and consume, and the cars we drive do have an impact on climate change, but the cause-and-effect relationship between the micro and macro is not as obvious to people on a day-to-day basis, despite the evidence. The coronavirus pandemic let us see the almost immediate cause-and-effect of our individual actions; for example, ignoring social distancing rules led to local and national restrictions that damaged the economy, whereas the feedback loop of our consumer choices on the environment have taken years to realize.

So a second hope for this book is to help organizations gain greater awareness of the connection from the micro to macro, the individual to the whole. There's a choice of systems approaches for doing this and I've selected the Six Lenses of Systemic Team Coaching to achieve it. I hope that our experiences during the pandemic have cemented our acceptance about the business case for a systems approach.

You will notice that I've not spent a great deal of time describing processes in any part of the book, whether in the Agile frameworks chapters or in the coaching approaches chapters. It's not that I'm not a fan of processes. I recognize the importance of processes and tools, but we have plenty of books on those, and no doubt your clients have met or are working with many highly experienced and well-paid consultants to help with those. You will be more effective as a coach, and your clients will get more value out of their investment into Agile frameworks, if we work with people to develop new ways of thinking and relating to each other. I believe this is the value of coaching, and it is what Agile Coaches should be doing. The context in which Agile Coaches work is specific processes and tools, but working slavishly to processes and tools sounds an alarm that people have stopped thinking for themselves.

I have a favour to ask: if you enjoyed any part of this book, will you write a review on Amazon, please, in light of the following questions? How does this book help you understand what it means to become agile and the role that you as a coach have in enabling that in organizations? What insights did you gain to help you use coaching skills to help your teams and colleagues become agile? What did you notice about the success factors for Agile frameworks that you can introduce in your organization?

In many ways, writing a book about agility is very un-agile. While writing, there were no feedback loops that involved the customer. After months of hard work, and sense-checking my thinking with trusted coaches, friends, and thought leaders, the work is unleashed to the world. I'm keen to involve you in further discovery of how the tools are being used, what has been useful, and what I've left out. Join the Community of Practice for *Becoming Agile* at futurefocuscoaching.org.

A note about the case studies presented in this book. My intention was to extend my own experience with examples from practitioners in a range of settings. I have attempted to present their thoughts and words as accurately as possible to what they generously told me at interview. There was no selection process on my part to present a viewpoint that I agree with, or which I may believe exemplifies an agile mindset and behaviours. I leave you the reader to make up your own mind about how you would work in similar situations.

# Acknowledgements

I am grateful to the people who gave advice freely on the writing process, and for reading early drafts and giving feedback: Teresa Leyman, Emma Sedgwick, Dot Tudor, Elvin Turner, Julia Vaughan-Smith, Maggie Wyatt.

Thank you to the following for your friendship and support while I was struggling to write during the pandemic: Nova Ferguson, Teresa Leyman, Rania Roelofs, Maggie Wyatt.

Thanks to all of the people who allowed me to interview them for case studies, or for subject matter expertise: Dan Abel, Lyssa Adkins, Hazel Chapman, Linda Holbeche, David Morgantini, Jon Smart, David Taylor. And those who helped generously with case studies and asked to remain anonymous.

Then there are the people who helped in the production of this, my first book: Nick Robinson, for copyediting and support with the case studies; Laura Pacey and Clara Heathcock at Open University Press – thanks for your patience and feedback during the writing of the book; Hannah Kenner, formerly of Open University Press, for the coffee and conversation at a coaching workshop that led eventually to this book.

And my husband Dominic, who lived through the writing and production of this book every bit as much as I did.

# Introduction

Despite growing support for Agile frameworks of developing products, organizations' efforts to change their culture to become Agile are mostly unsuccessful. The values and principles needed to transform culture, described in the Manifesto for Agile Software Development (Beck et al. 2001), require behaviour change among the leaders and teams, and their stakeholders, who develop products and services in uncertain and changing environments. This is a book about behavioural change in people to realize the benefits promised by Agile development methods. It is a deep dive into the professional coaching stance of the Agile Coaching Competency Framework.

I use this Introduction to present Agile Coaching as a blend of coaching, mentoring, teaching, and facilitation, with experience in business agility or organizational change. I have argued for increasing professional coaching skills in this blend in order to support individuals, teams, and the organizations they work in to enable sustainable change. I have framed this in a systemic way of working – the Six Lenses of Systemic Team Coaching – to address the complexity of the organizations we work in, and to address the influences in the systems around the individuals and teams we coach.

When coaching in an Agile context, we can no longer avoid the impact of the systems to which individuals are a member. Often the focus is on teams, who bear the brunt of not only delivering great products and services in constantly changing environments, but are also now responsible for thinking and behaving in an agile way and managing the inevitable blocks to their progress.

This book maps the essence of Agile development – the values and principles of the Manifesto and the behaviours implicated by them – to professional coaching. Agile development practices were created in response to growing complexity and uncertainty in our project- and product-delivery environments. And the complex and uncertain business environments we operate in have only become more complex and uncertain. I think nobody could have predicted at the time Agile frameworks were created (as early as the late 1980s but really taking off in the 1990s) that their use as a tool to manage uncertainty in product and service delivery would grow to encompass the mindsets of leaders, the behaviours of team members, systemic coaching, product innovation, and changing organization structures, by breaking silos that stifle communication.

At the same time, I have seen an increase in the number of coaches entering professional coaching and a growing number of those wanting to add 'Agile Coaching' as a component of their practice. I think part of this is that coaches see a market opportunity, but more that coaches became coaches as a way to improve the world of work and people took up Agile Coaching as a way to improve the world of work in IT delivery organizations. We have known many of the leadership skills and behaviours in this book for several decades, but it took a revolution in the way IT projects are delivered for a groundswell of delivery experts to insist on new behaviours and skills. The behaviours and skills indicated by the Manifesto have been with us all along, but major disruptive innovation caused by advances in technology for all aspects of business operations and new digital business models have these to the front of everyone's agenda. If Peter Drucker were alive today, he would be happy to see that 'knowledge workers' are finally getting their due.

# Is this book for you?

This book is for coaches who want to understand the coaching skills needed to coach leaders and teams in complex and uncertain business environments, as well as professionals who are already working and identifying as Agile Coaches who want to add professional coaching skills. It is also for leaders in organizations that want to get the best from themselves and the people they need in order to help their organizations thrive and win in highly competitive environments.

It applies to any organization that designs, builds, or sells products or services in fast-moving, competitive, or uncertain business environments, for which one or more of the Agile development frameworks could be useful. This book will not teach you the fundamentals of professional coaching for individuals or for teams.

And yet there seems to be a sort of barrier to entry for professional coaches. If you will allow me to muse out loud, I suspect that it's something cultural, that software developers have a culture in their profession that is different to the cultures of the other professions. After all, most professional coaches are in their second career. They come from marketing, HR, sales, finance, and others. There's no doubt there's a certain language that Agilists use, owing to a technical background. I must admit that my own language and thinking have changed as I have become more professional coach than technologist. I still know and love the metaphors of software architecture, but my language adapts to use the words and metaphors of my clients too, whatever sector they're from. I believe it helps to speak the language of the people you coach, and so it should help to spend time with people in their business culture to understand how to relate to them better, if that's who you want to coach. Is it necessary to have worked as a software developer? No, but it helps to have come from that culture. I know people who came from IT project management who have transitioned successfully into coaching Agile teams. Interestingly, they are often people who became fed up with management telling them to be command-and-control managers and subsequently decided there was a better way.

This work is based on a combination of theory and practice, and is aimed at helping coaches develop professional practice. Therefore, I assume that its readers are professional coaches. For example, I do not aim to describe how to contract in coaching, basic behavioural coaching models, the benefits and importance of coach supervision, management of coaching engagement, commercials, or ethical practice. An obvious secondary audience – though no less important audience for this book – is people working as Agile Coaches, for whom professional coaching is one of the four competencies of the role. If you have picked up this book because you want to be more effective at helping your client change and realize success with Agile frameworks, then this book is for you. But it doesn't replace training in professional coaching, or continuous professional development.

Most coach training programmes, including the one in which I learned coaching initially, start with coaching individuals and gradually add working with teams and then addressing systems, and in fact the literature is mostly organized around these divisions as well. An early version of the manuscript for this book drew the same divisions between leaders, teams, and the organizational system in which teams operate. However, we know that most failed efforts of well-intentioned teams and team leaders to benefit from using Agile frameworks are the result of being blocked by organizational impediments. We know that organizations are complex systems, that the products we are building are complex, and the business environments we are operating in are complex. So in mapping the attributes of great leadership, the requirements of today's teams, and the coaching approaches to support them, I start Part 2 from a systemic perspective and I carry that on throughout in order to emphasize the interrelationships.

After an introduction to Agile Coaching here, I'll move to focus almost exclusively on professional coaching for behavioural change. If you're working as an Agile Coach, or a coach working with stakeholders who want to achieve agility and use Agile frameworks, it's almost certain that your work will draw on more than just coaching to help you to be successful in the domain.

## Coaching in the Agile context

The Agile Coaching Competency Framework from the Agile Coaching Institute was an early attempt to scope and define the role of an Agile Coach. Created by Lyssa Adkins and Michael Spayed, it's been extended and built upon by practitioners, and today it is our reference point for the current role definition of Agile Coach. Other early definitions of Agile Coaching come from Liz Sedley and Rachel Davies, Esther Derby, and Diana Larsen. While you may be approaching this book as a coach with no intention to wear the badge 'Agile Coach', it's useful to know the scope of the role and the part that professional coaching has in it.

The Agile Coaching Competency Framework proposes that professional coaching, mentoring, teaching, and facilitation are important skills in an Agile Coach's toolkit. It assumes that Agile Coaches have a solid Agile and Lean mindset and working knowledge of the principles and mindset of the family of frameworks that have come before now. And rounding off the model of coaching, there are three competencies that I describe as coming from our 'past lives' – in other words, before we became coaches. These are technical mastery, business mastery, and transformation mastery.

# Agile Coaching Competency Framework

The framework is based on four competencies and four areas of domain mastery. The competencies are skills, whereas the areas of domain mastery come from your professional experience before becoming a coach. Agile-Lean practitioner is a prerequisite for all Agile Coaches, whatever your strengths.

**Professional coaching.** The ability to act as a coach, with the client's interest determining the direction, rather than the coach's expertise or opinion.

**Mentoring.** The ability to impart one's experience, knowledge, and guidance to help grow another in the same or a similar knowledge domain.

**Facilitating.** The neutral process holder that guides the individual's, team's, or organization's process of discovery, holding to their purpose and definition of success.

**Teaching.** The ability to offer the right knowledge, at the right time, taught in the right way, so that individuals, teams, and organizations metabolize the knowledge for their best benefit.

**Technical mastery.** The ability to get your hands dirty by architecting, designing, coding, test engineering, or performing some other technical practice, with a focus on promoting technical craftsmanship through example and teaching-by-doing, plus expertise in Agile scaling patterns or structures.

**Business mastery.** The ability to apply business strategy and management frameworks to employ Agile as a competitive business advantage, such as Lean Startup, product innovation techniques, flow-based business process management approaches, and other techniques that relate to innovating in the business domain.

**Transformation mastery.** The ability to facilitate, catalyse, and (as appropriate) lead organizational change and transformation. This area draws on change management, organizational culture, organizational development, systems thinking, and other behavioural sciences.

**Agile-Lean practitioner.** The ability to learn and deeply understand Agile frameworks and Lean principles, not only at the level of practices, but also at the level of the principles and values that underlie the practices enabling appropriate application as well as innovation.

(Agile Coaching Institute 2017)

When I teach Agile Coaching, I describe a 'dance' that good Agile Coaches practise when picking skills from this framework, when working in service to others. Professional coaching, while it can be used as an approach to encourage people to think for themselves, is easier to deliver credibly, I believe, when coach and coachee share a common language, frame of reference, and context. There are also anecdotal reports of coaches moving to specialize in niche areas. To be useful to clients, we must know when to use coaching, mentoring, training/teaching, and facilitation to help our clients move towards their goals.

The learning outcomes for the Agile Coaching course of the Agile Coaching track from ICAgile makes reference to the possibility of various stances in Agile Coaching, and to date I am not aware of any other large-scale attempts at setting standards for Agile Coaches. I suspect that more organizations will enter the space and attempt to claim part of it as their own, as we have seen with the various professional bodies in professional coaching.

# Professional coaching

To make the distinction between Agile Coaching and executive or leadership coaching, Agile Coaches often refer to 'professional coaching' as a competency alongside mentoring, facilitation, and teaching. To me professional coaching in this context has the most value when used to empower team members to think for themselves. Sometimes that means coaching leaders to give teams space to do that. Agile frameworks such as Scrum and Dynamic Systems Development Method (DSDM) say that having empowered teams is a critical factor for being agile. In other words, if you want to get the benefits of iterative and incremental development, you need to empower people, and mainly team, to think for themselves. When people think for themselves, they take ownership and work together proactively to find solutions to problems. The team acts as the 'engine room', using DSDM's description, working faster and with better quality than individuals can. Never has there been a more important time for empowered teams, which Agile frameworks promote.

Coaching is primarily about asking open questions to stimulate thought and promote a coachee's self-reliance. The coach follows the person's or group's agenda. That is to say that the coachee's needs or issues are on the table for discussion – not the personal needs, issues, or desires that a coach might have. Experienced coaches know this is easier said than done. The coach uses skilful questioning to elicit answers, options, and possible solutions. Coaching conversations in the Agile development context are usually about performance improvement and can include interpersonal issues, leadership style, thinking processes, managing difficult emotions, authenticity, building confidence, addressing imposter syndrome, and balancing work and personal/family commitments.

Coaching is seen by many people as a powerful tool for increasing performance because when the coachee takes responsibility for the agenda, they are more responsible and committed to their success. I often describe this as standing on their own feet or thinking for themselves. This is what we mean when we hear phrases like self-organizing teams, self-managing teams, or empowered teams.

# Mentoring

In contrast to coaching, a mentor shares their experience and knowledge to check understanding and stimulate thought and learning. Information is offered from the mentor's own experience to reassure and support individuals and groups.

It therefore follows that mentors are usually more senior. Self-directed learning is more limited, and self-reliance builds more slowly than with coaching.

A mentor's focus is on providing the group or individual with the knowledge to fulfil the agile tasks in hand and meet the requirements of the task or project. Mentors can encourage the exploration of thought processes to identify possible solutions and discuss appropriate behaviours for a context.

Mentoring has its merits over a coaching approach in some situations. They include when someone is at risk of making an unsafe decision – for example, a crisis moment; when a simple yes or no answer is needed; or when your coachee simply can't find the answer themselves because they haven't yet developed the expertise. Guidance on giving advice to a mentee comes with a warning about choosing carefully whether to give advice. Many Agile Coaches are seen to have earned this role through years of experience gained on the road to being recognized as an expert. We owe it to our clients to allow them to take ownership for their learning and to get all of the benefits of thinking for themselves. As technical experts – if that's how we started our journey to Agile Coaching – we were rewarded for providing solutions. As coaches, we do our clients a better service by withholding our solutions and letting them do the thinking.

## Facilitation

Like the other stances mentioned, facilitators get out of people's way. They do it so much that good facilitators can do their job without being at the centre of attention. Facilitators manage a process for the team to do the work they set out to do and made explicit in the meeting agenda. They also manage group dynamics and use themselves as an instrument to detect the unconscious forces at work that help or hinder a group from getting its work done. A facilitator has a toolkit of processes that they combine, through preparation that takes place well before the event. Processes selected by a facilitator might help a group to identify dependencies, recognize learning, make a decision, identify options, brainstorm, commit to process improvements, or improve their communication and dynamics. In addition, a facilitator encourages and agrees with the group behavioural norms that are needed to help the team to the work in the time allowed.

The facilitator sometimes needs to mediate in group conflicts and offer either interventions or a way forward, as appropriate. As part of thorough preparation, the facilitator also solicits input to the meeting agenda and agrees such input before the meeting, which ensures that the right people have been invited and that invitees know what they are expected to do and contribute. They provide feedback on the group's progress, often by summarizing both what has been done by the group so far and the group's progress towards achieving the meeting objective. Through skilful questioning, and being adaptable, a good facilitator challenges individuals' and a group's thinking and actions. The benefit of good facilitation is that a group task can be made easier by helping the group get the work done in a specific timeframe. This is especially useful for groups that seem to spend hours discussing things but never making decisions, that invite too many people with little accountability or responsibility for outcomes, or in organizations that think they have an inclusive process for making decisions but that ultimately leave it to someone senior to cut through a room and decide on others' behalf. When decisions are made in an inclusive and democratic way, a group takes ownership for decisions made – and the organization typically gets better decisions as a result of increased input from employees.

Part of your preparation is to design a lightweight process that lets the team do its work so that everyone's preconceptions and habits – including our own – can get out of people's way so that the work that needs to be done can be accomplished. Then be prepared to change your plan during the event. Thinking on your feet is the name of the game and plans are there – as in Agile projects – to get feedback on what's changed from what you knew at the start, not to hold the group ransom to your agenda. No doubt you have some experience of facilitating groups in either your pre-coaching management career, or as a coach or trainer. Use all of your coaching skills to be mindful of how everything that you do, from designing the process to your body language and behaviour – your presence in the room – helps the group or hinders them.

I steal good ideas from others, and you should do that too. Great books that I use again and again are *Facilitating with Ease!* (Bens 2018), *Facilitating Groups* (Rogers 2010), and *Psychology for Trainers* (Hardingham 1998) because they balance a discussion of processes and tools with the unconscious forces at work in groups which could derail any workshop; and *The Surprising Power of Liberating Structures* (Lipmanowicz and McCandless 2013) and *The Fifth Discipline Fieldbook* (Senge 2010) because their processes rise above the task of helping a group get work done to helping create meaningful dialogue and understanding of the people and systems we work in. Some expert remote meeting facilitators have come to the forefront during the last year and I've interviewed one of them, Judy Rees, and encourage you to think about what you'll take away from her approach. I'll draw on some of my favourites from these resources and others in later chapters of this book. Creativity as a facilitator is in trying new processes and tools to help groups do their work, and not in what you say or how much subject-matter expertise you have. Reflect at the end of the facilitated meeting or workshop on whether the group got or didn't get the benefits of the facilitation you designed; then why or why not. Tailor the processes and make them your own. Invent new ones. This is what learning in Agile product development teams is all about, and as coaches we should do this too.

What work needs to be done is, of course, context dependent. As a coach, I like to think about the *quality* of the interactions involved in the decision that needs to be made, if it is a decision, plus the resulting benefits of less agreement or more agreement to people's commitment and the resulting longevity of focus on the work to which people have committed. Now I'm thinking about facilitation as a coach, and not just as a person who knows where the markers and flip chart are located.

Facilitation, while not coaching, may be useful for helping the team to establish norms, such as listening to each other to increase trust, empathy, and psychological safety. They are part of the toolkits of coaches who work with groups. Facilitation, while distinct from coaching, is essential to a coach's work with teams for learning (Leary-Joyce and Lines 2018). While often described as a separate skill that is distinct from team coaching, I believe that facilitation is a skill that must be part of everyone's toolkit if you work with groups. And it's essential to do it well to help a team move up the stages of group development to high performing. When done well, facilitated meetings help promote dialogue among team members, help team members learn how to listen to each other, and create space for formal learning events, such as Sprint Retrospectives, which generate take-aways that are then followed up on. When done poorly, facilitation is used by command-and-control types to drive results using constricting processes and leading questions that disempower the team.

# Teaching

Teaching or training is primarily about giving information or telling, with some asking to test understanding. Teachers or trainers focus on filling identified skills gaps and providing best-practice tools and techniques, following a pre-agreed course outline or lesson plan. The focus is on specific tools activities, behaviour, or knowledge to improve effectiveness with Agile frameworks in hand. The purpose is to transfer skills, and it is usually implemented by someone internal or external to the organization, preferably someone with expertise in the topic, and who has a training qualification. Expertise does not indicate an ability to deliver great learning events; in fact, it is not a prerequisite, although a trainer must look and sound credible.

Most of what we deliver as Agile Coaches is better described as training, which usually includes facilitation and can include coaching and mentoring to a lesser degree. I propose that great training uses a combination of all of these stances, with an emphasis on teaching. Designing activities that are led by training participants, with boundaries and a clear task set by the trainer, encourage them to interact with the information delivered and make it their own. Experiencing the new skills or information – even if the activity is only a small-group discussion on a good open question – is miles more effective than delivering slides and lectures. I propose that the most effective teaching puts learners in the driver's seat. Trainers still need to design activities well, so that the learning objectives and tasks are scoped clearly, but the best learning takes place when learners stumble through the new skills with trial and error, and when they do so by stumbling through it in groups.

Approaches like *Training from the Back of the Room* have become popular among Agilists; however, even before Sharon Bowman wrote that book in 2009 and before it became popular among Agile Coaches, trainers in all subjects designed ways to get their students to 'do the work' and learn through doing.

There doesn't need to be a named framework for trainers to be effective at getting out of the way of learners and park their urge to show expertise. This trap – demonstrating expertise – holds back many people and the organizations that sponsor them from becoming competent Agile Coaches. In our previous careers as technical experts, we were rewarded for expertise. Each of us who comes from a previous career in tech needs to ask ourselves how easily we're going to transition to a profession that is about facilitating learning and move our knowledge and expertise, which we worked for many years to acquire, over to one side to make room for others to learn. The cruel paradox is that often the buyers of Agile Coaching want us to demonstrate knowledge and expertise to earn credibility quickly with the people we would coach.

Teaching is the least empowering of all of the skills above; nevertheless, part of an Agile Coach's role is to teach Agile frameworks such as Scrum. You'll see many references to Scrum in this book because, in my opinion, it encapsulates better than any of the other frameworks the human behaviours that create conditions for success with Agile development. Others that may be of interest, which you would need for your Agile Coach toolkit, are Extreme Programming, or at least a working knowledge of Continuous Integration and Test-Driven Development; Lean Startup, including its iterative learning cycle and the true meaning of minimum viable product; Kanban, including work in progress limits and queues; DevOps, which is making projects and project managers obsolete; DSDM a pragmatic project management framework, which integrates seamlessly with Scrum; and Design Thinking, often overlooked as an Agile framework, its human-centred design approach is a hand-in-glove fit with Agile development approaches.

As this is a book about behavioural change to achieve business results, this is primarily a book about the professional coaching stance. We don't need to have skills in all of the competencies mentioned above to be good Agile Coaches. My own opinion is that it's not possible and not practical to try to do all of them well. Some people don't have the energy to facilitate a training for one, two, or three days. Others lack experience with mentoring because they haven't been in the role with a mentee or don't identify as a mentor, even if advice is given appropriately. What Agile Coaches seem to have in common is a strong preference for professional coaching skills, or at least an aspiration to learn those skills. And the governing bodies that have stepped into the Agile Coaching space seem to agree. For example, the International Consortium for Agile, or ICAgile, includes Agile Coaching in two of its learning tracks. Trainers of the Agile Coaching (ICP-ACC) course must be accredited coaches.

## Check your motives

We've all come from other careers before deciding to become coaches, and in our previous careers we may have been required to use more of a consulting style, or more of a teaching style, or we may have used mostly mentoring skills. Being a coach of Agile leaders and teams will challenge your old habits, and old tendencies, to fall back on 'telling' behaviours. Some of the hiring managers who look for Agile Coaches don't want to know that coaching is a long game. Becoming truly agile and changing both mindsets and behaviours in order to be successful when using Agile processes requires putting choice into the hands of our clients to make the change. That means we need to use our professional coaching skills often. Unlike in a one-to-one professional coaching session, which may last for one to one and a half hours, it's not always so clear when we are using coaching skills, mentoring skills, facilitation, or teaching. We don't have the luxury of a clear separation of 'ask' and 'tell' behaviours as we have in one-to-one coaching. I have come across many practitioners with the title Agile Coach, as I'm sure you have, who do more telling than asking. We need to be clear in our own minds about the motivations, needs, and competing interests that may require us to choose one approach over another in the moment. Our self-awareness therefore needs to be greater when working as an Agile Coach.

When I started my coach training at Henley Business School in 2014, each of us had an opportunity to be observed as the lead tutor for feedback; that was worth gold at the time and it still is. My feedback was that I appeared to be active during the short coaching session – active in the sense that I was thinking more than being receptive to what the coachee was saying and therefore wasn't really hearing him completely. After observing myself in coaching sessions, I realized I was thinking of solutions to the coachee's issue – something so fundamentally opposite to the purpose of coaching and so automatic for me after years as a technology consultant. I still catch myself thinking of solutions, but it takes a second or two for me to intercept that habit, instead of the ten or twenty minutes it took when I first started coaching.

A delegate on one of my three-day Agile Coaching courses asked me, 'So how do I get that manager to do what I want?'. His question missed the point and revealed to me that for many people, coaching is seen as another component of one's toolkit for influencing – some would say coercing – people to 'do Agile'.

One client who I worked with in an Agile context made clear that 'weaponized Agile' was being used in the organization, and suggested strongly to me that such an approach wouldn't be tolerated from my coaching work. To me, this demonstrates a risk that the nascent Agile Coaching profession could be viewed as a tool in the weaponry of people who would otherwise find ways to influence through coercion and political manipulation in order to change minds.

Coaching can be a long game. Despite what some coaching programmes assert about structuring coaching sessions to demonstrate results from session to session, we know that people need time to integrate new skills, and the change that us coaches desire to see so badly in our clients while we're working with them may not take shape until after our work together finishes. Change must germinate and take hold in the decisions of individuals. Therefore, those calling themselves practitioners of Agile Coaching who seek instant results are choosing the wrong profession.

# Empowering leaders

Success with Agile frameworks rests on behavioural and cultural change in organizations as a result of its links to a set of values and principles (Rigby et al. 2016). Whether called team leaders, Scrum Masters, project managers, Agile Coaches, or any other facilitative leader whose actions are emulated by teams, leaders working in these environments must promote behavioural change. I believe that facilitating this change falls to the domain of coaching to support teams and the wider organization for the reasons cited earlier in this chapter.

Agile Coaches attempt to bridge the gap between the so-called 'traditional' management mindset and the Agile mindset by developing Agile teams. Their work, according to an Agile Coaching Institute white paper on Agile Coach competencies by Michael Spayd and Lyssa Adkins (2011), is part coaching and facilitating, part teaching and mentoring, part industry knowledge in Agile and Lean methods, and part domain experience: experience of the business context, technical environment, and organizational change.

The role of Agile Coach has developed considerably during the last ten years; however, little academic research has been done to prove the efficacy of Agile Coaches to facilitate the change that is needed to complete agile transformations. Adkins wrote in 2010 that Agile Coaches need to work on self before coaching others; however, there is little evidence of how teams and organizations transform through coaching interventions.

By 2014, little research had been done on the importance of Agile principles on successful outcomes (Bermejo et al., 2014). Some academic literature says that success with the principles leads to success with using Agile methods in the organization (Dikert et al. 2016). A study by Williams (2012) surveyed a university community's view of Agile principles. She said that most people responded that the principles were important to guide people new to Agile frameworks, and that teams should select working practices that agree with the principles.

When thinking about team objectives or organizational goals such as business objectives, we need to think about how the group works – together as well as individually – in order to get the group's needs met. This is why systems thinking is important – to see the group/system in such a way that we know how to modify our behaviour to make the team or organization effective.

Whatever your role, you have the choice to lead by giving advice as an expert or bringing the right people together to co-create solutions to your tough problems. Bill Joiner and Stephen Josephs, authors of *Leadership Agility: Five Levels of Mastery* (2007), describe the adult stages of personal development relevant to leaders, based on a field called stage development psychology.

Most adults, Joiner and Josephs say, live at the Expert and Achiever levels, but few adults move beyond Achiever. However, to develop the kind of collaborative work we have described as necessary in uncertain and changing environments, leaders must move beyond problem-solving ability and a strong sense of their values, purpose, and other factors that create their identity. A small portion of adults reach beyond these so-called 'conventional' stages of adult development to three 'post-conventional' stages: Catalyst, Co-Creator, and Synergist.

Joiner and Josephs used it as the framework for their research into the impact that leaders can have at each of the five adult levels. The impact areas or 'action arenas' they defined are for leaders to hold 'pivotal conversations', exercise 'team leadership', and demonstrate 'organizational leadership'. As a coach, you may find it useful to use the five leadership levels and the three action arenas as an alternative to the 360 Feedback tool that's often used at the start of coaching engagements.

Perhaps not surprisingly – although it should not be overlooked that their work provided important evidence of what we all suspected – they found that as leaders developed behaviours and emotional capacities at the higher levels, they also developed the ability to manage change, uncertainty, and complexity more effectively. The most successful leaders, the authors found, showed four competencies that helped them succeed in the most turbulent environments, across five agility levels.

While their examples of each of the five levels make fascinating reading, and they could certainly be part of any Agile leadership coach's assessment criteria for leader maturity in complex environments, the authors' Leadership Agility Compass applies to team members – who many would say exercise leadership every day anyway – as well as people in leadership roles.

A summary of the primary four competencies in the Leadership Agility Compass by Joiner and Josephs (2007) is:

- *Context-setting agility* involves understanding the complexity in the external business environment as it relates to potential or real impact on your company's ability to thrive. You must be able to turn uncertainty and volatility into strategic initiatives and be able to describe expected outcomes to your line of business. This competency relates to Lens 6 of the six lenses of systemic team coaching, a framework I'll return to.
- *Stakeholder agility* involves skill at building relationships with people you need across lines of business, business units, and functions in order to gain support for your initiatives and projects. This competency relates to Lens 5.
- *Creative agility* involves employing techniques for seeing problems in new ways and engaging your teams to exercise creativity on tough business problems so that you don't need to come up with all the answers yourself. This competency relates to Lenses 3 and 4.
- *Self-leadership agility* involves developing reflective capacity to learn from past performance and observe yourself in the moment. This competency relates to Lenses 1 and 2.

In the remaining sections of this chapter, I present coaching tools that you can use when working with leaders in complex environments. I selected the areas based on my own experience of working in organizations and my coach training and for the MSc in Coaching and Behavioural Change; the areas were sense-checked against Joiner and Josephs' work. I'll return to these four competencies throughout the book in the reflective questions. Note that each competency is represented in the Six Lenses of Systemic Team Coaching.

# Empowering teams

Coaching empowers team members to think for themselves. An empowered team is the 'engine room' or 'supercomputer' that can work faster and create more innovative solutions than individuals can. And product development initiatives often require teams to work at their highest level of creativity and flexibility.

The enduring definition of a team is from Katzenbach and Smith (1993), and you'll see elements of their definition throughout the advice given where teams are concerned, in the form of cross-functional teams (complementary skills), clear understanding of the business need (common purpose), defining a Sprint goal for each timebox of work (performance goals), and self-organization (mutually accountable).

Leary-Joyce and Lines say in *Systemic Team Coaching* (2018) that facilitation is part of the work of a team coach. Working with teams to understand their relationships in the system requires that you are able to work to a professional facilitation standard, including the ability to reflect on your relationship with the group as you support team members in understanding both the systems in which they work and the important relationships. Systems practitioners must at the same time manage themselves, how they engage with the team, and the context in which the team operates, and they must know at the outset if their role is as a member of the system of interest or as an outsider (The Open University 2020).

For Ingrid Bens, whose book *Facilitating with Ease!* (2018) has the kind of paradoxical title that belies the challenges of good facilitators described in her book, a facilitator attends to the explicit processes that he or she designs to help the group do its work, and also attends to unconscious psychological processes through both observation of others and keen self-awareness.

We've stated that good facilitators have self-awareness and design processes to help a group achieve its tasks. When working with groups online, we must add keen self-awareness of our facial expressions, tone of voice, and tactics for engaging people when using video conferencing tools. These are in addition to what I've said here about good facilitation. I will elaborate on the intentional behaviours that work with groups in the Lens 3 chapter.

Therefore, I propose that our understanding of the relevance of facilitation is expanded greatly beyond facilitated timeboxed meetings; for example, the Scrum Master's role as a facilitator. Scrum Masters and other team leaders still need to understand, however, that effective facilitation still makes room for the team to do its work without explicit or implicit suggestions about what work to do or how to do it.

This book does not claim to help you design a team coaching engagement, but it does present coaching approaches that work well for teams working in uncertain and changing environments. If you've not discovered them already, please look at the work of David Clutterbuck, Peter Hawkins, and John Leary-Joyce and Hilary Lines for guidance on contracting and using other tools for designing a team coaching engagement.

# Developing a systemic lens

Working systemically is about working with wholes, and about interrelationships. For people who have found success with breaking down large issues in order to solve problems systematically, thinking systemically – the opposite of working systematically – may be challenging. The Six Lenses model offers a way for us to see the whole system in terms of human relationships in order to understand our product development team's dependencies for success. Successful change efforts depend on coaches seeing (and helping their clients to learn to see) the layers of the system, or interrelationships, and pick up on what people pay attention to in order to design coaching interventions. Leary-Joyce and Lines illustrate the six lenses in *Systemic Team Coaching* (2018).

Inspired by the short coaching story in *Systemic Team Coaching*, I've written my own scenario set in an Agile context to help bring the lenses to life. The scenario is based on my work as an Agile Coach in an organization where I engaged with individuals, teams, and a sponsor. Later in the book, when I present case studies of individuals discussing their organization's Agile adoption efforts, I'll ask you to identify the speaker's attention to various interrelationships according to the Six Lenses.

## The Six Lenses in an Agile context

The following scenario is based entirely on a real experience while working as an Agile Coach. I've not used the real name of the individuals, and I've withheld the name of the client. These short summaries will be reproduced at the start of each chapter on the Six Lenses.

---

*Lens One – Individual*

*I was asked to work with a business analyst to help him understand and address what the sponsor described as 'problems fitting into the team'. When meeting the business analyst, who I'll call Brian, I found him to be quite open to meeting me, because first and foremost he expressed interest in learning new things to expand his professional skills. His expressions, body language, and choice of words and intent expressed high emotional intelligence. This was clear to me from the first few minutes of meeting him. I felt clear at the time that this was not a case of a charm offensive, charisma, or telling me what I wanted to hear. This didn't seem to be the same person who had been described to me by the sponsor. Brian relayed to me some of his frustrations about his role as it was seen by others in the business unit, and he was eager for me to meet his line manager to help me understand a wider perspective on the issue.*

*Lens Two – Interpersonal*

*I met with Brian and his manager, who I'll call Tanya, to discuss some of the feedback he'd received, and the stated reason for the coaching. (Note that*

---

*Tanya was not the sponsor for the coaching engagement.) What I observed between Brian and Tanya was good rapport and a great deal of respect for Brian's position and quality of work by his manager, Tanya. Whatever impressions some people in the business unit had about an issue with Brian's interpersonal skills were not reflected in this relationship. Tanya described Brian's effort to change the way the business analyst role was viewed and showed support for his desire to improve 'the way things are done around here'.*

Lens Three – Team tasks: Purpose and objectives

*I had the opportunity to observe several teams' Sprint Planning meetings while working with this organization, including the team of which Brian was a member – before I was asked to meet with him one to one. As a product development team, the team members had a clear purpose (to build a software service that would perform a strategic business function of which they were all aware), and in this meeting they were focused on planning work for the current Sprint. However, there was no clear Sprint Goal defined that would allow team members to select items from the Product Backlog that they could use to achieve the Goal. Instead, I observed the project manager reading a list of items sequentially from a Product Backlog and asking for these next items to be assigned to team members, with an on-the-spot discussion of the technical tasks that individuals would need to complete in order to do the Product Backlog Items. I noticed a few anti-Agile behaviours and practices that would hinder any team, whatever processes they employed, Agile or not.*

- *The work for the Sprint did not have a stated relationship to business value because they had not defined a Sprint Goal at the start of Sprint Planning.*
- *There was no self-organization to discuss how the team would achieve the Sprint Goal. Tasks were self-assigned and individual names were recorded by the project manager somewhere.*
- *There was no collective ownership of the work due to not having a team plan (Sprint Backlog) that would be owned by the team.*

Lens Four – Team relationships

*My impression of Brian's work with the team during one Sprint Planning meeting was as a facilitative member of the team who proactively sought clarification from team members, attempted to summarize what he heard, and make sense of the implications of what he heard, greatly benefiting everyone else in the team. It is important to mention that the team was split across two geographic locations and met over a teleconference, and some team members spoke English as a second language. In this type of environment, miscommunications tend to be more frequent than when team members are co-located. Perhaps unknowingly, Brian fulfilled the facilitative role of an Agile business analyst extremely well to help the team better understand the business problems and features under discussion. The team's project manager/Scrum Master was running the meeting by working down a list of tasks that she assigned to the team for the Sprint. In this type of environment, miscommunications tend to be more frequent than when team members are co-located. Personally and privately, I questioned the strength of the relationships among team members if so much communication was mediated by the business analyst and the project manager.*

*Lens Five – Stakeholder interfaces*

*Brian described differences in other people's view of his role, specifically that the purpose of a business analyst was seen by his department as being different to his view of what was needed from the role to support the team. He described a sense that others did not value his contributions as much as they should have. Through informal conversations, I learned that the staff reporting lines were quite separate among the project managers, business analysts, and technical roles such as testers, developers, and architects. Each entity seemed to be working to different organizational objectives, and indeed I discovered later that the measures that each group worked to were different.*

*Observation of the team's project manager showed a command-and-control leadership style, task-level management, and driving the conversation with the team instead of Agile-style facilitative leadership. This indicated that the business unit favoured a management style that was focused on the delivery of tasks instead of outcomes. My observation about the project manager correlated to what I had learned and observed about the business analyst through our conversations, and in his interactions with the rest of the team.*

*Lens Six – Wider systemic context (PESTLE)*

*The client organization, which I will not identify, operates in a highly competitive market that is subject to price fluctuations caused by the availability of refined natural resources, seasonal consumer demand, regulations and intense competition, some from low-cost entrants during the last ten years. Operating in a highly volatile, competitive, and uncertain market likely put senior management under tremendous pressure to deliver projects on time.*

## Conclusion

Taking a systemic perspective using the Six Lenses showed a more complex picture of the issue that produced unwanted behaviours from employees, in this case from a business analyst. Agile Coaches should seek to develop the lenses and facilitate discussions with people relevant to each perspective so that all parties can understand where their behaviour helps or hinders the organization in achieving its business objectives. This is a way of seeing interrelationships that provide a richer picture of behaviours that help or hinder a team. Developing your way of seeing in this way will help coaches design interventions more successfully than focusing on individuals or teams in isolation. In Part 2, I offer a framework for addressing organizational change and a workshop facilitation approach for addressing culture change.

### Conversation with Lyssa Adkins

I'm grateful to Lyssa Adkins, co-creator of the Agile Competency Framework and author of *Coaching Agile Teams*, for our conversation in June 2020. We talked about the need to improve professional coaching skills in Agile Coaching and the challenges that coaches are facing when working with organizations that want to become agile.

Laura:  The book is aimed at existing coaches who are looking to add to their skills to understand how to work with people to become agile.

Lyssa:  That's super-great, because there has been a needed bridge between the professional coaching world back into the Agile world.

Laura:  The book is about one-to-one coaching as much as teams because leaders have so much influence.

Lyssa:  I know, and they're in so much pain. They're just really so caught, so I'm glad you're doing that work with them. I'm doing more of it now too.

Laura:  If you were to write a second edition of *Coaching Agile Teams*, which is now ten years old, what would you add? What would be in the second edition?

Lyssa:  You know, I haven't actually looked at that book in a very long time and it's just recently that I got the go-ahead to record the *Coaching Agile Teams* audiobook. So I am reading that book with a fine-toothed comb. I am marking it up like a piece of music because I have to deliver it now in a story-like engaging fashion and many people have said, 'Are you going to write a second edition before you record the audio book?' Because as you say it is ten years old – it was ten years old just last month, on May 31st. So happy birthday to the *Coaching Agile Teams* book. As I read the book, the thing that keeps coming to my mind is the phrase 'and I really meant it'. There are perhaps things that I use now in replacement. For example, the conflict model: typically, I use a different conflict model now than the one in the book, but the one in the book is sufficient. So the things that I would update are very minor for this book.

Now the Agile world has advanced to the point that this book and many other books are needed. So your book is needed and both books still work together. The *Coaching Agile Teams* book is the book that broke open the attempt to start to define Agile Coaching and started to create a way for people to know how to be on the right path to develop themselves.

Laura:  And I see the book as being about self-development as a coach and also about attention to the blend of competencies that is required. So the Agile Coaching Competencies shows coaching and mentoring, teaching and facilitating as being distinctly different. But I noticed that you call the coach competency a Coach-Mentor role. That's because you say that professional coaching in this context includes processes and a really defined mindset.

Lyssa:  Professional coaching is not the main course for an Agile Coach. It's a side dish. It's a part of what Agile Coaches do, but not the whole thing. Now Agile has advanced to the point in the last ten years that you could have a team of coaches come into an organization and you could have some professional coaches that are only working on things that a typical executive coach would work on with people, but you would also need people who are Agile-Lean practitioners to help people know how to use Agile in the workplace. For most people, being Scrum Masters or doing Agile Coaching no matter what their role is called, all four of those skill sets of teaching, facilitating, coaching and mentoring (plus there is giving advice and mentoring), all of those are needed and at different volumes or different levels, depending on the situation at the moment.

Laura:   Absolutely. And so [in this book] I'm trying to frame that in a way that sits right with me being true to myself [as a coach] and also pays respect to that foundation of the four competencies.

Lyssa:   This is the application of professional coaching in a specific context. It's really not that different from managers who want to be more coach-like, who use professional coaching with their direct reports, and then there's that moment where they have to be a manager and say, 'Yeah, so sorry, here's the corporate "answer" to the topic we're discussing'.

Laura:   We still need business processes.

Lyssa:   Yes.

Laura:   It's the kind of mindset I think, and the underlying principles that people want to race past still to get to tell me what to do: 'What's the right answer?'

Lyssa:   See, I think why the *Coaching Agile Teams* book is selling more copies in the last six months than it has in any other six-month period, even though it's ten years old, is because all those basics got raced by. They'd been raced by in the last ten years, everyone took a glancing look at how Scrum works. They said, 'We've got this thing'. Then they ran into all these organizational impediments of course, because most of them weren't using Scrum well. They would have run into them anyway, but if they were using Scrum, well, they would have had a lot more information to help business leaders make different decisions about impediments. So we are where we are now; so advanced books are needed and the first book that people read on a subject is also still needed.

Laura:   It is, very much so. So I suppose the way that I've been able to focus my book to make it valuable on the bookshelf next to yours is by focusing on behavioural change and that means professional coaching. So I see this book as a deep dive on the professional coaching needed to become agile.

Lyssa:   I love it. You know in the Agile Coaching Institute, we used to have a course that was a deep dive in professional coaching. There are the four competencies and a deep dive into professional coaching, which is where people's hearts and minds can change for good.

Laura:   And in a sustainable way.

Lyssa:   That's exactly what we were after. When all the consultants leave the building, can these people continue working this way?

Laura:   And have they adopted the mindset, the acceptance of change, okay with 'not knowing'?

Lyssa:    Yes. All the things that we're helping people develop, as you listed, especially in this pandemic era, are certainly really good ways to cope with modern life.

Laura:    So tell me a little bit more about the areas where you're working with clients now and any anecdotes or short stories, if you can.

Lyssa:    I'm in a big like persona change right now, because my identity has been so closely fused with the profession of Agile coaching for the last ten years and my work has been training, developing, and coaching Agile Coaches for most of that time. So I haven't been on the ground coaching teams for a very long time, and in the meantime, while I was doing all that work training and coaching other people, I was getting a whole new depth of skills in my professional coaching skillset too. Those are things I really want to use and the place I want to apply them is with leadership teams and boards of directors.

        So that is the thing that I have started to move into. I have my coaching skills, but also a complement of tools that I use to help leaders understand the shift they need to make and it's not at all the same thing or the same way that delivery teams or middle managers need to shift. So that is the work that's on the horizon for me.

Laura:    I get the sense that you're aware of some problems that need to be solved at the senior level.

Lyssa:    Yes. The work I've done has so far proven my hypothesis about the work that needs to be done at that level. It turns out that it's really similar to the work that needs to be done at the delivery team level, because it's almost hardly ever about the executives not having enough information or not being analytical enough. It's almost always about their human system dynamic and their ability to communicate, make decisions, and make decisions stick in groups.

Laura:    It's obvious to me and you and almost everybody else that it's the interactions, our relationships, that are so important, as well as our ability to expand our mental model.

Lyssa:    I agree. The main body of coaching knowledge that I'm drawing on is organization and relationship systems coaching from CRR Global. That's the type of professional coaching that I'm certified in, which is how to coach the group as its own entity, so that's one. I've recently taken some introductory work and I'd like to do more with Caitlin Walker from the UK; her work is around clean language coaching and systemic modelling. This is basically helping people express to one another their mental models of how they think about things, how we're thinking about approaching this decision together, or how we think about what's happening. The other piece I'm picking up these days is somatic coaching, because I'm starting to really understand the wisdom in one's body – myself personally – and I'm starting to see that significant and sustainable behaviour change is going to require that component. And I'd say there's probably just two more.

        One is integral facilitation; I took a certificate programme, a year-long programme in that, and that's basically how to help a group stay in conversation, stay in flow when there is significant difference.

Either a really hot difference or a really cold difference, but there's significant difference and conflict. The final thing is The Leadership Circle Profile assessment, which helps leaders understand the shift they need to make to move into the VUCA (volatile, uncertain, complex, ambiguous) world and also to be a match for Agile, because Agile was built for the VUCA world.

Laura: The issue of professional standards comes up over and over again.

Lyssa: It's a real issue. It's not true that if someone has an ACC from the International Coach Federation, they are a great coach. Now it is true that they've done a pretty big ball of work to get there. In my case I was in a really intense programme and we did become good coaches, otherwise we couldn't get that designation, but that's not true of all pathways.

Laura: And if the standards are varied and not very well defined for professional coaches, then what about Agile Coaches? Is there more standards work needed at the moment? ICAgile has probably, as far as I know, the best-defined standard. On the Agile Coaching course I deliver here in the UK, I have people who take the course and don't aspire to that expert level of competency badge. They go for the Agile Coaching course and they get the knowledge-based certification and deploy it into their organization. What's needed here? Am I making too much of it?

Lyssa: You're not making too much of it. The standards exist and I'm really happy with how the ICAgile organization has held the standard. The ones associated with courses are, as you said, education certifications. They say you've got some knowledge. ICAgile has a competency-based certification at the top. The gap is that there are not many organizations creating the programmes like we have in strong professional coaching skill pathways. Those programmes would feature practice and assessments to rigorously help people move from 'I got the knowledge' to 'I'm actually skilled in this'. More will be coming online because ICAgile has just decided they're not going to allow people to go through the pathway on their own any more. They have to go through a competence-based certification programme in order to achieve the ICAgile Expert level, because the people who were taking the class and then practising on their own for six months or more were not able to pass the competency assessment level. The failure rate was just huge and I think that's because what we're talking about with the skills, especially if facilitation and professional coaching are so counter-cultural to how most people have operated in their work life up to this point, that it's not as simple as just, 'hey, I'm going to get the basic veneer of listening and asking powerful questions down and then I'm good'. It's not as simple as that.

Laura: So are there any improvements? Is there any good news in people's development of an Agile mindset or understanding of the principles? Where do you think there's good news?

Lyssa: I think there's tons of good news. First of all, ten years later, we no longer have to talk about why professional coaching skills are useful for Agile Coaches. That is a done deal and so many Agile Coaches have gone off to get professional coaching training, and many of them even certifications because they knew that this thing that we touched in these Agile coaching courses had a very deep lineage and a very deep set of skills. So that is all really good news. I think what's also good news is huge external forces that are affecting us. The younger generations coming into the workplace have a mindset that is more in concert with Agile.

I think the other thing that's really positive is that no matter how people want to ignore it or sweep it under the rug, the world is increasingly volatile, complex, ambiguous, and uncertain. There's no way really to escape it for very long. Agile and the coaching that comes along with Agile is perfect for helping people not only barely hanging on by the skin of their teeth, but actually have a sense of autonomy and agency in the midst of all of that uncertainty. To even thrive in a lot of cases.

Laura:   Absolutely. I feel a little bit like this is a book that doesn't need to be written because so much of what I'm writing about is about increasing human agency to deal with change and labelling it. Agile is a little bit redundant, but perhaps as you say, these approaches need to be put together into one volume.

Lyssa:   You know, I've always thought about Agile as a really good excuse, because so many of the things that come along with Agile, like professional coaching, leadership development, all that stuff was always good advice and good things to do in organizations before Agile came along. With Agile in an organization, its main job is to show impediments. So those impediments get thrown in people's faces again and again. As a result, leaders go off to do some work on themselves, perhaps using a tool like The Leadership Circle 360 assessment. They understand how they have to move from reactive to outcome-creating actions, minds, and hearts. It's painful for them every day if they don't do that, not only because of Agile, but because of the forces of VUCA. So Agile is a great vehicle to ride in.

As we move further into an age of disruption, which I believe we are moving into, I would love for all of us Agilists to be thinking about how we contribute to alleviating suffering and to working with things that are likely to be highly traumatic, like climate disasters and perhaps more pandemics – any host of truly global crises. I've been thinking for the last year about the question of what could we Agilists do that could be helpful to people making the hard decisions, for example about how to respond during climate disasters. So I'm really interested in the musing of 'what if all of this Agile in organizations has just been practice ...'

Laura:   For something much, much bigger.

Lyssa:   For something much, much bigger and much more important for our survival and thriving as a whole species.

**Reflective questions**

1 Where are your strengths in terms of the Agile Coaching Competencies? Thinking about a team that you've worked with or are working with now, what balance of skills among professional coaching, mentoring, teaching, and facilitating did/do you need at the start of your coaching engagement? What skills might you need to use six months into your work, twelve months into your work with the team?

2 Reflecting on the interview with Lyssa Adkins, what should be done to improve professional coaching standards for Agile Coaches? What part do you have in making that happen?

3 Thinking about the work you have done prior to becoming a coach, are your skills strongest in technical mastery, business mastery, or transformation mastery?

4 Recall an individual you worked with in a coaching relationship. To which of the Six Lenses did you and your coachee give the most attention during the coaching work?

# Part 1

# Agile Foundations for Coaches

# 1 Origins of the Agile mindset

**Why you should read this chapter**

- Agile frameworks and techniques may seem like a fad to some people; however, they have their origins in leadership and management practices and systems thinking, which are not new and which will be familiar to many coaches.
- To work with your coachees to change behaviour, we need to understand the theoretical and practical origins of the Agile frameworks our clients choose to use.
- By appreciating that what has come before Agile frameworks were defined by software developers, we tie organizations' desire to gain the benefits of using Agile frameworks to a much wider body of knowledge in order to help us in tricky moments.

Agile frameworks got their start in the late 1980s and 1990s, and were broadly called 'iterative and incremental development'. We didn't think of these alternatives to the traditional project planning methods as 'agile' until seventeen software developers met and wrote the Manifesto for Agile Software Development in 2001 (Beck et al. 2001). They emphasized a process of breaking down work into short timeboxed iterations to deliver an increment of a product or service that has immediate value, followed by re-prioritization of the remaining work. By 2001, these seventeen industry leaders met to discuss the progress they'd made in improving the profession of software development. Each person represented a worthy approach that provided an alternative to the traditional way of delivering projects (known colloquially as waterfall delivery), whereby all of the development work is started, separated from testing, and a workable product is not realized until the end of the project lifecycle. The result of their meeting, at a ski resort in Utah, was a statement of four values and twelve principles that they held in common.

I see Agile frameworks as being a progressive evolution from the principles and mindset of Lean, with stark similarities in all but name throughout Extreme Programming, DevOps, Scrum, DSDM, and Lean Startup. The latter, Lean Startup, is attributed to Eric Ries, who wrote the book *Lean Startup* (2011), which is descendant from Lean thinking and is applied to startup companies. DevOps pays direct credit to lean and continuous delivery, particularly to the ideas of flow and 'stop the line', or empowered people. Scrum's founders were inspired, at least in part by Nonaka and Takeuchi, two researchers and proponents of Lean management.

# Lean

You'll see Lean principles throughout this book, as so much of the Agile mindset, frameworks, and practices originate from Lean, originally called the Toyota Production System, defined primarily by Taiichi Ohno and Shingeo Shingo in the late 1940s.

Agile frameworks borrow liberally from Lean – its principles, mindset, and practices, originating at Toyota, have been woven into the fabric of agile working; for example, Kanban, just-in-time planning, and elimination of 'waste' from the production system.

Mary and Tom Poppendieck provide a useful, succinct primer on Lean for people in software development in their book *Implementing Lean Software Development* (2007). The Toyota Production System (TPS), on which Lean Manufacturing and Lean Product Development are based, has two pillars, according to Taiichi Ohno in his book about the TPS ([1978] 1988): just-in-time flow and autonomation. Both of these pillars are visible in the Agile frameworks in use today, including Extreme Programming – better known now for the practices TDD, continuous integration, refactoring, and others – Scrum, DSDM, and DevOps.

Also known as small batch sizes, just-in-time flow – or just-in-time planning – originally referred to the movement of inventory or goods through the manufacturing process. In software development, the arena in which most organizations will use Agile development methods, batch size refers to the amount of work in progress – or feature size – that the team commits to developing and delivering. It is analogous to 'minimum marketable features', which is the language sometimes used by Scrum teams to describe the next most valuable item to develop for customers. Just-in-time (JIT) flow was created as a way to reduce waste brought on by overproducing parts or products that became outdated or unwanted because something in the market changed. The antidote to increasing profits through economies of scale was to produce as little inventory as possible – and have as little partially done work as possible – so that if the market changed, or a defect was found in inventory, the plant could change focus with minimum waste. The complexity of today's global marketplace, make it very difficult for most organizations to predict what it will need in the future. Somewhat paradoxically to some people, JIT teaches us that it is best to commit to as little as possible at one time – small batches of work – in order to respond quickly to unpredictable changes and ultimately deliver more value to customers and to adapt quickly.

My interpretation of autonomation is 'empower the team'. The common definition of this is 'stop the line'. In software development terms, it means repetitive tasks are automated and workers, or team members, are empowered to take immediate action when a defect or bug is found. They don't assume that someone down the line is going to test and fix issues, effectively deferring responsibility and potentially making the fix of problems more complex and costly.

## Continuous improvement

You can think of Scrum as a continuous improvement framework, in a way. Continuous improvement was used heavily at Toyota in Japan, which was also the birthplace of Lean. Edwards Deming introduced it to Taiichi Ohno at Toyota decades ago. This is where we get Lean. So actually, if you go right back to the source, it's actually the Deming Cycle – plan, do, check, act – and you'll see this in the Scrum framework.

# Servant leadership

While it's not a new idea, servant leadership, or facilitative leadership, has appeared on people's lips more recently as a result of the Agile leadership style promoted by Agile frameworks. The phrase 'servant leader' will not be new to anyone with a basic understanding of the Scrum framework. A well-known description of the Scrum Master role is servant leader, teacher, and coach. Users of Scrum may be surprised to learn that the phrase was not invented by Scrum – it was defined by Robert Greenleaf who wrote in 1970, 'It begins with the natural feeling that one wants to serve, to serve first. Then conscious choice brings one to aspire to lead' (Center for Servant Leadership 2020). It is not, he said, the desire to rise to a position of power or wealth. Servant leadership, or 'servant-first leadership', is marked by attention to others' needs above our own. The needs he referred to are similar to needs to self-actualize and to grow as people. The aims are similar to those found in humanistic psychology. Abraham Maslow (1943) wrote about self-actualization as the highest order motivation in his hierarchy of needs; Carl Rogers ([1961] 2004) believed that therapists could help their clients increase agency for change through their own resources.

Dan Cable wrote in the *Harvard Business Review* (2018) that servant leaders create the all-important culture of learning that is the key to growing a team's capability. I think of this personally as engaging with everyone I meet with the attitude, 'How can I help you today?'. I might say it aloud or keep it to myself, but I try hard to think how I can support and enable other people. One of my core beliefs as a coach is that people perform best when they think for themselves, and that being in service to other people's autonomy is good for my business. I think that in order for anyone to believe that servant leadership and the autonomous free-thinking that follows from interacting with others in that way is a good thing, you need to trust people to make choices for themselves. Cable (2018) calls top-down leadership 'outdated, and more importantly, counterproductive' and says, similar to Greenleaf and Maslow, that to get the best work from people they need to have purpose at work. Clearly, the purpose must be created and understood by teams through skilful communication from leaders about the organization's mission and objectives.

# Feedback loops

Agile frameworks, recognizing the need to embrace uncertainty and ambiguity to be successful, have, in effect, made it the norm for companies to change direction through feedback. The newest of the Agile frameworks, Lean Startup, puts learning at its core by advocating that product development teams experiment by creating 'minimum viable products' to real end customers that maximize feedback and learning (Ries 2011). The types of products the teams are developing are characterized by complexity in the business requirements, a wide choice of development tools and how to utilize them, design and implementation choices, the competitive business environment in which the organization operates, and the time-to-market demands by consumers.

The Toyota Product Development System, on which Lean Software Development is based, is an empirical approach with deliberate feedback loops to help the designers adapt to refine the design concept. This has an uncanny resemblance to Scrum's timeboxed Sprints, and DSDM's Development Timeboxes, which set a cadence of learning how to adjust to evolve both the product and the team's practices to be more effective.

As with most modern management approaches, Agile development methods are built on and borrow heavily from a combination of past management approaches and management theory. On the theory side, much of what we know about the wisdom of feedback loops has been codified into systems thinking since the 1990s, originating from the natural and social sciences, engineering, and management theory (Senge 2006). The systems thinking mindset, wrote Peter Senge in *The Fifth Discipline* (2006), is concerned with seeing the relationships between things in a system, and sees change and adaptation as being structured of conceptual feedback loops that show change as being gradual, and influences as many different but related factors in the system. To influence the system, he said, you need to pay deliberate attention to what the system is telling you, particularly the structure or process of the underlying system at work.

DevOps also recognizes the concept of feedback loops to get evidence, often of the effect of small changes. The emphasis is on checking small changes, otherwise known as frequent testing, as in XP's continuous integration. Problems are easier to fix when they're small and when they're identified as close as possible to the time that we humans make the mistakes.

### Feedback loops in systems

Senge says there are two types of processes at work in systems: (1) reinforcing, or amplifying, processes, and (2) balancing, or stabilizing, processes. Reinforcing processes are more easily thought of as virtuous cycles and vicious cycles. An example of a virtuous cycle given by Senge is of a student who is praised by their teacher for good work on one assignment; the teacher's praise motivates the student to do more good work and they earn more praise from the teacher. This could have easily gone the other way: if a student does poorly on an assignment, for example, there may be problems at home, leading the teacher to consider the student an underachiever and leading to poor motivation on the part of the student. Clearly, this is an example of a 'vicious cycle'. The point is that in each example, the student became great or not from a series of interactions, not a one-off incident in either case.

Balancing processes try to maintain the status quo. Balancing processes have a goal or target that the system aims for. One of Senge's examples is of a driver of a car whose goal is to get to the store. Along the way, she must give way to other drivers and move out into the centre of the road to give room to a cyclist. Senge says there are many examples of this in organizations and gave an example of a friend's training organization, whereby employees were burned out. The leader of the organization tried to get people to work shorter hours, but employees just took work home with them, because the organization's culture – based on the example of the leader – was that to get ahead you had to work long hours.

Behaviours that reinforce an organization's culture are examples of a system trying to balance itself. In the case of culture, the goal or target is unconscious; however, it is very present, nonetheless. We saw that in Senge's example of his friend's training company.

Learning about what is taking place in the system accelerates when the time between each action and reaction is relatively short. Senge calls this a 'delay'. The shorter the delay, the quicker one can observe and learn from changes in the system.

### Process and project adaptation

Research on effective teams outside the arena of Agile software development emphasizes the need for teams to improve continuously. Team coaching support is a way to help teams learn by doing. For product development teams, including software development, teams reflect to generate new knowledge that results in improved products, processes, and services.

The abilities to learn how to improve product increments through feedback and improve the team's practices through continuous improvement are seen as essential to successful product development in today's marketplace. The most recently created approach in the Agile family of methods, Lean Startup, emphasizes learning as the central tenet of the approach. By building the smallest version of the product idea, and releasing it to the organization's target customers, the organization maximizes feedback and therefore learns about what their target customers want.

# Continuous learning

All of the Agile frameworks have in common continuous learning, often represented as feedback loops. Feedback here does not refer to the one-to-one conversation you have with your manager, for example. It's more subtle than that and must be planned into your team's working practices in order to make it visible. It has been called a process of turning tacit knowledge into explicit knowledge (Nonaka and Takeuchi 1996) in order to recognize experience that can be poured back into working practices. Peter Senge is famous for his learning organization theory and much of the Agile practices draw on that work directly, as in DevOps (Kim et al. 2016), or indirectly, as in Scrum, which is heavily influenced by Nonaka and Takeuchi's work (Re Turner 2018). Scrum's Sprints make continuous learning a ritual in the Sprint Retrospective. As coaches, it is our job – on a daily basis – to look for signs of a team lacking these qualities, without waiting for a facilitated meeting to look for them.

## Senge's four core disciplines

### Personal mastery

Senge calls this the pspirit of the learning organization' (Senge 2006: 131); it can be defined as an individual desire to learn and grow continuously. It is not dissimilar to Carol Dweck's learning mindset or Maslow's belief that the highest human motivation comes from self-actualization, which brings together intense personal purpose and the company's purpose. To create the learning organization that Senge said was so important to a highly effective business, its people must strive for personal mastery. As with so many aspects of our work as coaches, personal mastery requires working with and seeing our current reality while working with creative tension. Personal mastery is building learning capacity, as opposed to new knowledge or power. Its true power lies in the difference between where a person is now, and where he or she aims to be. The 'to be' vision could be a personal, team, or organizational vision.

Indentifying, structural blocks – or limiting beliefs in the coaching world – are the bread and butter of good coaches. Senge says that acknowledging our limiting beliefs and their origins by being truthful to ourselves when we notice them creates an as-is or current reality that then gives us a starting point for working towards the vision. As a coach, you will have worked with your coachees on identifying the current reality and options for reaching a future goal many times.

People I've worked with who have high personal mastery say things like, 'the more I learn, the less I realize I know about that subject', 'other people must know more about that than me!', and 'the list of things I want to learn keeps growing; there's not enough hours in a day to learn everything'. When people are hungry to learn, and they are in an environment where they are allowed to simultaneously learn for personal and corporate aims, a leader can back away from micro-managing.

### Mental models

Coaches will readily recognize a mental model, or map of the world in NLP terms, as a lens through which each of us sees the world and makes decisions for interacting with it. It's built from our experience, including experiences from our childhood of which we most likely did not have any control or awareness.

Our mental models filter information that to some may seem obviously import-ant, but to us it may not ever register if it disagrees with our beliefs about how the world works. Adapting our mental models so they are fit for purpose for our organization's challenges is key to helping us adapt. In the face of evidence of needing to change and adapt, organizations with the smartest people will ignore the facts so as not to contradict what they know in their heart of hearts to be true. Our job as coaches is to help organizations develop skills to change mental models. Use your reflective practice skills with your coachees to help them learn how to gain awareness, or as Senge says, to be truthful about their mental models.

### Shared vision

A shared vision, Senge said, is 'a force in people's hearts' that unites all of the activities and tasks that people are working on across a team or organization (Senge 2006: 192). It unites people to a common purpose and drives people to achieve more long-term goals, which reinforces the vision. The virtuous cycle continues unless the understanding of the company's shared vision is under-mined by competing views of how to achieve the vision, which creates dissen-sion. Unity around a shared vision can lead to *generative learning* – the expansion of our learning capacity. In other words, we are driven to learn how to learn better. When we work doggedly in pursuit of our shared vision, we demonstrate courage, Senge said. Courage is of course one of the values of Extreme Programming and of Scrum. A shared vision provides the context for all of our decisions, often referred to as the 'why' of this programme or initia-tive. An organization can lose commitment to its vision when individuals don't believe that they can impact the environment in which they work. In his presen-tation *The Path to Agility 2010* (2011), Ken Schwaber recalled examples of how Scrum's adoption was hindered. He said that when he and Jeff Sutherland created Scrum, he expected teams' ability to develop great software product to shoot up, but they failed because, among other reasons, they didn't feel empow-ered to do so.

### Team learning

Team members work together and can adapt without having to coordinate con-sciously. High-performing sports teams, and improvising jazz musicians, are two of the most often cited examples of this. Effective team learning, Senge said, has three ingredients: thinking deeply about complex issues, team collab-oration and clear coordination, and advocacy of team learning practices by an organization's team leaders. Alignment of purpose seems to be a success factor, as it is in so many other contexts: 'Team learning is aligning and developing the capacity of a team to create the results its members truly desire' (Senge 2010: 219). Many team coaches do team-building events, or very effectively conduct visioning and purpose workshops for their sponsor, but the benefits of creating a shared vision, and using team learning to turn the team into a true 'engine room', as DSDM describes development teams, are lost if team members aren't able to have effective dialogue and listen to each other with respect. As opposed to having a discussion, in which an individual seeks to have their viewpoint strengthened and accepted, dialogue involves exploring all viewpoints. Critically, this means we need to be aware of our assumptions and judgements and leave them to one side in order to understand others. This is where skilled facilitators can be of great benefit to a team, as an independent facilitator can listen carefully to identify assumptions and judgements in the moment.

# Complex systems

At its essence, this is a book about helping people manage through change in complex organizations. So why wait until now to mention complexity? Like Senge's core disciplines of the learning organization, complex adaptive systems (CAS) is another systemic way that Agile Coaches use to think about interrelationships in the teams and organizations they work with.

The mindset we need for managing through complexity in business is often attributed to David Snowden. There are other approaches to complexity coming from other disciplines. I find complex adaptive systems too abstract and cognitive for use in coaching; to understand and ultimately improve human interrelationships, I seek to develop empathy and compassion. This skill seems to come from other parts of the body than the ones I use for CAS thinking.

Nevertheless, you'll come across Snowden's work being referenced often among the IT crowd, perhaps due to Snowden's tech background. He's a professor of complexity science and originally created the Cynefin framework. It means place or domain. This is about our ability or inability to predict outcomes based on existing knowledge and, despite our best efforts, to control outcomes. The 'situation' can be about managing a requirements list on a project or anticipating how a new product will be taken up by our target market. Snowden's work on complex adaptive systems is referenced often by Agilists, and you will see it come up all the time in blogs and training courses, like the new silver Nissan Outlander that you just bought, which now seems to appear everywhere you go. However, to work as a coach to help people adopt an Agile mindset and behaviours, you don't need to be an expert on complex adaptive systems. You only need to know that in organizations, teams are systems, and so is any organizational unit, and even the company itself. And every person in any of those systems influences the systems of which they are a member, in unpredictable ways. In your work as a coach, you will work with your clients to understand other ways of identifying the systems in which people work.

Working in complex environments means that things are not always what they seem. It is not possible to break down problems into their parts, analyze the parts, and expect to come up with the one right answer to help us prioritize work for months ahead on a project, or build the best product that will clobber the competition. This is partially due to the systems we work in being made up of humans, who each see the world differently. What this means on a practical level is that the problems we're addressing at work do not have predictable solutions, partly due to the inherent problem of not always being able to see the problems or agreeing amongst your team on the problems to solve.

Complexity exists in the system in which teams and organizations operate, but there is also complexity in the work itself, brought on by the wide choice of platforms and tools for software development, the need for novel solutions or a bespoke implementation, or product differentiation. Sometimes, that product complexity is the result of management relying on an old mindset of grouping like-minded people with similar cultures together, as in business functions. Many in IT have argued that a siloed organizational structure on the product development efforts produces siloed product design and, as a result, systems that are poorly designed and difficult to support and change. The complexity and resulting unpredictability are thus in both how we work and the work itself.

Various models, frameworks, and approaches attempt to help us see the complexity, uncover helpful and unhelpful behaviours in our relationships in the organization, map situations, and offer solutions. One framework that I have found useful is McKinsey 7S, from the 1980s. It encourages a holistic view of any change effort, for example a transition programme, a cultural change, or the implementation of new product design or project management approaches. While it wasn't proposed explicitly as a systemic approach to understanding organizational change efforts at the time, it is a form of sense-making that I employ when working with groups to help them get a holistic view. Seeing complexity can be much more difficult than seeing the design of a software system or organizational structure. The most challenging complexity in systems comes from not being able to see past our own maps of the world. This is where coaching can help.

I recall a recent webinar that I wrote and presented on Agile leadership coaching. A Q&A question from one of the participants who joined using the webinar platform was, 'What do I do to change the mindset of someone who has a fixed mindset?'. My first response: 'How do you know the person has a fixed mindset?'. With much of one-to-one coaching, the situation can be understood when the issue is owned by your coachee, and from there your job is to help your coachee create greater awareness of that, generate options for possible solutions, and commit to trying one of those options. But in complex organizations, your coachee's issues are most often situated in the organization, and so they are influenced by people in the system in unpredictable ways. The relationships your coachee has to others in the system are relevant, as is the ability to see the relationships.

## Systems approaches

Senge and Snowden are explicitly mentioned by Agile practitioners as having an influence; however, the influences of other approaches are relevant. Keep an open mind and look outside the usual suspects referenced in the Agile development literature; for example, systems dynamics, whose leading proponent, Jay Forrester, suggests making sense of systems by using balancing and reinforcing feedback loops instead of straight-line cause-and-effect models. Stafford

Beer, the founder of systems science, or management cybernetics, said that business problems could be solved best with interdisciplinary teams. He also acknowledges that groups can solve their own problems – echoes of Scrum's self-organizing, cross-functional teams with all the skills necessary to develop a product, and DSDM's definition of the team as the 'engine room' where creative problem-solving occurs. Soft Systems Methodology, created by Peter Checkland, is a widely used modelling approach for understanding complexity in business organizations. His background in project management and experience with late-running projects will resonate with many Agile development practitioners. Soft Systems Methodology encourages practitioners to model their view of reality to challenge existing views, so that new understanding of a complex problem can be created in the process. To be effective at this, we need to be open to accepting others' viewpoints and to accept continuous learning through inquiry. And finally, one of the most influential thinkers about systemic thinking in management, Russel Ackoff, identified new ways of understanding human systems, called Social Systems Sciences, which broke from the established Operations Research approach in the Second World War. In Social Systems Science, he advocated for a more expansive and inclusive approach to understanding problems, instead of a reductionist or analytical one that only looks at a system's parts. He said that modern management practice requires managers to manage their employees' interactions instead of their work. Learning, he said, only takes place through experience (The Open University 2020). He asserted that organizations must record mistakes and learn from them, engaging in regular course correction, like an airplane through a hurricane. He believed that systems thinking was the only way for people to overcome resistance to change.

---

### Reflective questions

1 What feedback loops did you notice in a project in which you learned along the way how to adjust your approach? What were the examples of feedback you received to signal that you needed to improve skills, modify tooling, or change your approach in any other way?
2 In what ways do you as a coach model reflective practice for your coachees?

# 2 A coach's perspective of Agile methods

**Why you should read this chapter**

- When starting a new coaching engagement with an organization, the leaders and teams you work with will expect you to be familiar with the Agile frameworks they've invested in. The market is saturated with books to help you learn the processes, roles, and practices of Agile frameworks, but as a coach you'll need to understand the mindset of each.
- Our clients' use of Agile frameworks often shows up as specific language coming from one or more of the frameworks and techniques mentioned in this chapter.
- Much has been written about the roles and processes of each, but to coach in an Agile context you also need to understand the principles and mindset.

The ambition of this chapter is to present the most commonly used Agile frameworks in such a way that coaches can understand the value of them in terms of mindset and principles. As I learned Agile frameworks sometime in my career in software delivery, I approached them in the way that most people do – as processes to follow. As I worked more with Scrum and Kanban while working as a software consultant at British Airways, I started to wonder why the team wasn't getting the desired results. It became clear quickly that there was no magic bullet as a result of having our Daily Scrums, and I started to look at how the team was organized, what the team was working on and when, and how the work related to our Sprint Goals and the software project's business objectives. When my career moved into professional training and coaching, I started to see the origins of the approaches, what they had in common, and the success factors for teams using the methods. As my coaching matured, I started to think more deeply about the values and principles and how different teams in their own context expressed those values and principles. I accepted that 'what good looks like' for Agile frameworks is not the same for everyone – Mike Cohn has said there is no 'best practice' in Agile, and that was profound when I read it. Success depends on whether the people using the methods are conscious of what they need from their investment in using them, what they expect to happen in developing products using them, and their courage in looking at what helps or hinders them. This journey is similar to what I see my clients experiencing.

The following is a rough sketch of the journey of mindset that I see my clients experiencing, in parallel to my own evolution of thinking about what

'Agile' is about. As our thinking about Agile frameworks matures, so does our courage to allow people to think for themselves.

> **Scrum** – level 1 – process to follow; level 2 – team behaviours and values for empowering them to do their best work; level 3 – a framework for building habits of reviewing our practices and learning from each other.
>
> **Lean** – level 1 – tools to gain efficiency; level 2 – learning to see wholes; level 3 – empowering workers to achieve excellence.
>
> **DSDM** – level 1 – a project management lifecycle; level 2 – principles of engagement for senior project stakeholders; level 3 – a planning mindset that emphasizes learning from experience.
>
> **Kanban** – level 1 – a task board; level 2 – a capacity-planning tool based on flow; level 3 – a tool for revealing organizational impediments, and for team self-organization.
>
> **DevOps** – level 1 – a toolset for continuous testing and deployment; level 2 – silo-less working to achieve cross-organization collaboration; level 3 – an environment that supports innovation and experimentation.
>
> **Extreme Programming** – level 1 – a set of progressive development and test practices that break the waterfall habit; level 2 – a way to welcome continuous feedback and improvement; level 3 – a management philosophy that allows people at every level to do their best work.

While it's impossible to present all of the currently used Agile frameworks in this book – there are already several primary sources which I've referenced – the purpose of this chapter is to present the frameworks and approaches at the level of mindset and principles so that coaches can work with coachees more effectively. I don't promise to short-cut the work it takes for you to develop expertise in these approaches, or even to communicate the methods' core processes and techniques.

One of the reasons coaches tell me they want to learn Agile development is so they can use their professional coaching skills in organizations that are adopting Agile frameworks, and they want to look and sound credible. To me that means that we use the same language as those we are coaching. That's what this chapter is for, in part, but it's about more than that. This chapter will help you understand the fundamental concepts underpinning the way Agile teams complete work. When you go to work with your client sponsor and the teams in the organization, they may not be aware of these themselves. You may therefore find yourself in an Agile Coaching role and teaching these to your client. Hopefully, you'll be modelling these in the way you work with your client. For my own part, I have found that the way I complete work for my business has changed over the last ten years or so, as I progressively came to understand the Agile mindset and practices at a deep level. I still need to remind myself that perfection is a killer of progress.

In summarizing the currently used Agile frameworks here, my aim was to help to further explore the Agile mindset in each of the frameworks and approaches, and help to eliminate the 'cargo cult' mentality that wants to copy and follow rules but not to internalize learning. Despite the growing adoption of Agile frameworks such as Scrum, we are still seeing many organizations slavishly following the very lightweight process indicated in the framework. I become speechless when asked by team leaders and team members questions such as, 'How else is the Scrum Master supposed to find out what the team is doing unless they attend the Daily Scrum?'. The pitfall with the type of thinking indicated by that question is that organizations have replaced wholesale what they have done in the past with the new-new thing, in this case Scrum, including anything that might have been working well. They continue to ignore the same advice given by traditional project management approaches that asks a project team to tailor the delivery method to the complexity of the product they're building, the environment they're working in, and the customer's quality expectations.

This is why I've not described the processes of the methods in this chapter. You can find those yourselves. A better use of these pages is to describe the principles to help in further developing an Agile mindset and, more importantly, to understand what I call the prerequisites for getting the most value out of an organization's investment in learning the method. Broadly speaking, when all of these methods are used to discover what's working or not in product development, you're getting your money's worth. Having the skills to do something about improving yourself or your organization is what this book is really about.

# Lean Software Development

As in Lean, Agile teams work to increase the flow of valuable products through their production process while minimizing waste to improve time to market. To get transparency into this process, and to identify wastes, we monitor and measure work in progress.

Poppendieck and Poppendieck (2007) defined seven principles of Lean Software Development, which I see as essential for creating a foundational Agile mindset. Look for them in the other Agile development methods presented in this chapter. They are all present in the other methods, whether or not they are named explicitly.

### Eliminate waste

Eliminating waste is about reducing the time it takes to get a new product or feature to market from the time a customer requests it, or when the design team creates the requirement. Reducing and eliminating waste shortens the time to market. With practice, in time you will spot examples of the seven wastes in most areas of life. To identify waste, you need to first be able to identify 'value' to your customer. Everything that is not valuable is waste. The following seven wastes of Lean are the adapted versions in Lean Software Development. I've given the original name of the waste from Lean Manufacturing for each, as I find it helps to hear the original name to grasp the true meaning.

*Eliminate waste 1: Extra features*

In Lean Manufacturing, this was referred to as Over-Production: over-development and attachment to features we don't need or want and poor due diligence on understanding the product's vision, user needs, and market opportunity, including features that are not needed in the current system. The worst source of waste in software systems is extra features. Why would a team build features that aren't expected to give immediate value?

*Eliminate waste 2: Partially done work*

Partially done work is the unfortunate result of big-batch delivery, long-term commitments, and teams that are organized along functional silos instead of cross-functional product teams. In Lean Manufacturing, this is In-Process Inventory. Breaking work down into small batches is one of the biggest sources of resistance to adoption – and therefore success – with Agile development in teams that ask for help with the transition.

*Eliminate waste 3: Defects*

The name is the same in Lean Manufacturing. It should be obvious why defects are waste; nevertheless, in some organizations they are negotiated like the bad debt that was packaged, traded, and ultimately led to the last financial crisis. Okay, perhaps I've used a bit of hyperbole here, but the point is that they don't go away and often come back to bite harder later. When a defect is found, write a test to be sure it doesn't happen again. Don't put off until tomorrow what you can do today.

*Eliminate waste 4: Delays*

So many of the wastes are related, with a waste in one category causing a seeming inevitable waste in one of the other categories. Delays are a great example of this, as they seem to be entwined with handoffs (waste 5) and partially done work (waste 2). When you commit to delivering features in big batches, with big handoffs to another team, it becomes much harder to predict when your product or features will be done. There is a delay while the testers wait for developers to finish unit testing their code, and in the meantime, because management do not want to see testers sitting around waiting for work to arrive, they are asked to work on somebody else's project or system. The product, in this example software, goes around and around in a loop from testers to developers and back to testers.

*Eliminate waste 5: Handoffs*

Handoffs, or throwing work 'over the wall' as it's known commonly, is the almost inevitable consequence of siloed working, where, for example, quality is the responsibility of the testers down the line. In Lean Manufacturing, this is called Transportation. Handoffs of large batches of work almost always result in people down the line being required to read documentation in order to learn about the partially done work that they've been given to complete. If you've ever tried to understand the decisions and creative problem-solving that have gone into doing any knowledge work by reading someone else's documentation, then you know how much knowledge gets lost.

### Eliminate waste 6: Relearning

In Lean Manufacturing, this is Extra Processing. This is also described as wasted knowledge. Failing to create opportunities to turn tacit knowledge into explicit knowledge, and failing to include people with the product knowledge into the product development process are examples of relearning.

### Eliminate waste 7: Task switching

Task switching has two definitions. It is multitasking, or what I call keeping plates spinning, whereby a developer has a few tasks to get done and is trying to keep them all in progress. I use an analogy in my courses of doing your housework on a Saturday morning. You're trying to do everything, but getting nothing done as a result. You're trying to do the vacuuming, and your husband is asking for help in the garage, the cat wants to be fed, and the delivery person is at the door requesting a signature. What will you prioritize to do first? But there is a more subtle meaning of task switching that goes right to the heart of the characteristics of software development and all 'knowledge' work. It takes time to get into a piece of work and hold in mind the complexity of the work before you can continue and know what to do next. For example, when writing this book, I've noticed it takes at least thirty minutes of getting re-engaged in the work before I'm absorbed in the work and making real progress. In Lean Manufacturing, task switching is called Motion.

## Build quality in

Defects happen, but when we identify a defect our efforts should be in finding ways to prevent them from happening again in the future, not in creating reports of defects or, worse, waiting for someone else to find them and report them to you. If you're not able to prevent the defects from occurring in the first place, test in very short cycles to identify and fix them.

## Create knowledge

I remember working in one of my first software development roles in the mid-1990s and being asked to write pseudo-code in technical design documents. My well-intentioned manager thought that if we all did this, and sat through a formal 'inspection' by the senior developer, that we'd get better quality software.

Guess how often my code looked like the pseudo-code written into those documents? Software development is complex knowledge work, which means it is impossible to predict how a developer will solve problems and create solutions to get the thing working. Ikujiro Nonaka describes the human processes that turn tacit knowledge into explicit knowledge in 'The knowledge-creating company' (Nonaka and Takeuchi 1996). He is also the co-author with Hirotaka Takeuchi of 'The new new product development game', published in the *Harvard Business Review* in 1986, which was the inspiration for the Scrum framework. Product development teams create knowledge by creating regular opportunities to reflect on the work that was done and recognize lessons learned. This is true for the evolving design and development of the product or system, as well as the team's processes and practices. This critical practice of creating knowledge is one of the team factors that create competitive advantage for a company.

## Defer commitment

Avoid making decisions too early, to leave open the possibility of change when change occurs. This can also be thought of as keeping your options open. By committing to less now, we loosen our attachment to specific outcomes in the future.

## Deliver fast

'We need to figure out how to deliver software so fast that our customers don't have time to change their minds' (Poppendieck and Poppendieck 2007). When I repeat this quote to participants on my courses on Agile development, I almost always hear a snigger coming from someone in the group. I have interpreted this to mean, 'Yeah, right. That can't happen here!'. When surveyed about the reasons for adopting Agile development methods by Version One in 2018, respondents said speed of delivery was their number one motivator. To achieve this as a leader, you need to empower people to make decisions without them waiting for you to make the decisions for them. Constantly improving your ability to catch defects early is also a big contributor to speed.

## Respect people

Based on three out of the four cornerstones of the Toyota Product Development System, the Poppendiecks expanded on what respect for people means in Agile organizations. Their definition of 'respect people' is based on these three cornerstones:

1 *Entrepreneurial leaders*. Great companies develop great leaders, which enables teams to build successful products.
2 *Expert technical workforce*. To maintain a competitive advantage, you must develop your own people to have expertise, instead of using suppliers and vendors for their expertise.

3 *Responsibility-based planning and control.* Trust teams to turn outcome-based plans into team plans that let people think for themselves about how to get the job done.

## Optimize the whole

To launch products to market faster, you need to examine the whole value stream – the process 'from concept to cash'. Organizations that attempt to address inefficiencies in getting new products and services to market, and which operate in silos, tend to address only parts of the whole value stream. Mapping your core value stream is important for identifying a cross-section of people who should be involved in any change efforts and product development initiatives. This book does not attempt to describe the processes and tools of Agile frameworks, but instead focuses on principles and values that indicate behaviours.

# Kanban

David Anderson writes in *Kanban: Successful Evolutionary Change for Your Technology Business* (2010), that Kanban was the tool defined by Taiichi Ohno in the Toyota Production System to see improvement opportunities in the kaizen, or continuous improvement process. He created the Kanban method around 2006/8, based on the Kanban pull system defined at Toyota, to get visibility of work in his software teams. The best description of Kanban that I can think of, described to me by my friend Ellis Bell, who also teaches Agile frameworks, is that it 'makes the invisible visible'. Unlike watching moving parts on a factory floor, it's difficult to get a single picture of where the inventory of software development work is located in the system. Look out across a room full of developers, and you'll see people with heads down at a monitor and keyboard, discussions in small groups, and the occasional, if not daily, check-in meeting. How close is that feature to completion? What's blocked? How much partially done work is outstanding? A Kanban board makes these things visible quite quickly.

Knowing the principles and other fundamentals of a framework are a prerequisite for getting value out of your investment in using it. Anderson's five core properties support Kanban's efficacy as a system for adapting to the unpredictable (2010: 17):

- Visualize workflow – this is achieved by representing work items on cards, physical (such as index cards or Post-it notes) or virtual (such as card representations on electronic, software-based 'boards').
- Limit work in progress – to deliver more, focus on less. Finish what you started, work in small batches.
- Make process policies explicit – everyone knows the rules of the system and they don't need to wait to be directed or be told what to do.

- Use models to recognize improvement opportunities – the models Anderson gives as examples in his 2010 book are the Theory of Constraints, Systems Thinking, W. Edwards Deming's concept of variability, and *muda*, or waste from the TPS. He notes that models from sociology, psychology, and risk management are being used with Kanban.
- Kanban is giving people permission to think for themselves.

My personal motivation for coaching Agile teams and my belief in the purpose of coaching are to enable people to think for themselves. Kanban brings this belief to life better than any of the other Agile development methods. Far from having rules and processes for people to latch onto, Kanban asks teams to start with wherever they are now, pursuing evolutionary change of their practices in order to deliver value to the customer faster and with better quality. If, as a coach, you observe a team looking to define the ideal process to model on its shiny new board (whether it's a physical board or software based), then please do everyone a favour and intervene straight away. Do not wait to speak up. Have the courage to say that the team is helping no one by copying a process that worked for someone else, for different products, in a different organizational culture and a different context entirely. As coaches we need to model helpful behaviours for others. Speaking up and taking action are part of a kaizen culture, or continuous improvement culture. Team members, like the factory workers the Poppendiecks described in Lean Software Development, are empowered to take action as soon as a problem is observed. To speak up and take action proactively, people have to work in a high-trust culture.

# Extreme Programming

The values, principles, and practices of Extreme Programming, or XP for short, were documented by Kent Beck in the 1990s to summarize the work of many people who took up the challenge of finding more effective ways of delivering software projects (see Beck 2005). In addition to Beck, Ron Jeffries, Ward Cunningham, and Martin Fowler are among the many passionate software developers who did much to advance the nuts-and-bolts practices of software development. The values, principles, and practices of XP have, to my mind, become the current definition of Agile, if Agile was a strictly proper noun, though most people don't use XP's terminology in favour of the current most popular kid at school, Scrum.

Beck cites Lean Manufacturing and Lean Product Development as a part of XP's heritage. As you'll see in the next section on DevOps, Lean and XP, together with facilitative leadership and a one-team culture of development and operations, were brought together to evolve XP into DevOps. The evolution took approximately a decade.

Software development teams follow the continuous integration practice, defined by XP in the 1990s, to ensure that new features are tested and validated in as close as possible to the time that developers do their work in, and call a feature done from a functional perspective. If any defects slip through the automated testing, the tests are enhanced without delay. This recalls the Lean pillar of autonomation, where tooling is used to assure quality in a reliable way, and workers are empowered to stop the line to fix errors straight away. When team members don't want to fix defects, Beck calls this 'a failure of values, not technique'. He says this indicates a failure of learning, or wanting to learn, how to improve the team's practices. To me it can also indicate an environment of low psychological safety, which must be present for people to speak up and say, 'This is broken and we made a mistake'. I say more about psychological safety in Part 2.

XP's five values provide a useful starting point for coaches to work with teams in order to help define what these mean for the team and what they look like in practice. In this way, you can help the team define its own norms quite quickly. By this point in the book, if you've been reading the chapters sequentially, some of these should start to look familiar. I've tried to capture Beck's take on each of them. He notes that each relies on the other to work effectively in software development:

- *Communication*: Communication is important for creating an effective team and building knowledge to both solve problems and to stop problems from recurring in the future.
- *Simplicity*: Going straight to the heart of Lean's small batches, this is about finding the most pared-down solution that will give benefit now or solve an immediate problem. It is what the team deems to be simple, based on their knowledge.
- *Feedback*: This is essential for adapting to change, and with more frequent feedback you can adapt more quickly and with less cost. Often associated with formal feedback given during annual reviews and similar meetings, feedback here doesn't mean the same thing. It's recognizing evidence for whether some part of our work was effective or not – for example, running tests and whether we met customers' needs. Actively creating ways of getting feedback – evidence that our idea or hypothesis is true or not – is essential in complex environments and is critical to team learning. 'Try it and see' is often the most rational way forward, but instead we often make the mistake of wanting certainty so badly that we commit everything to the first idea that comes along.
- *Courage*: Visible in several ways, courage includes taking action to solve a problem in the face of uncertainty, speaking up, and being brave enough to change course.
- *Respect*: Beck says this value is fundamental to the others. Every team member and all the stakeholders are important.

# Scrum

So where does Scrum fit into this? Scrum is one of the frameworks underneath the capital A when Agile is used as a proper noun. Despite what you'll hear from some people, Scrum and Agile are not synonyms. Scrum is a great starting point because it gives us guidance on the working environments and the habits of the team, which helps us to deliver on time, to be flexible, to gain focus, and to deliver quality work. It started as a framework to help software developers delight customers. There's no guarantee of success in Scrum, just the promise that if you're using Scrum you'll find out quickly what's working and what's not, so that you can do something about it.

Since Scrum was created in the early 1990s, references to Scrum as a software development framework have been changed to product development more generally because the world has caught on to the benefits of delivering in small batches. Software development isn't the only domain in which it is difficult to predict with accuracy everything that the business will need in a project or product development initiative. Moreover, our competitors, government legislation, and all of the sources of change we mentioned in the PESTLE model, create change that we can't predict, no matter how good a process we have.

## Scrum Masters

Much of this book is spent discussing capabilities required of leaders and teams. When we talk about leaders, many of you will be thinking 'senior manager', but you should also be thinking about leaders who have direct touch points with the team that delivers the products. When we talk about Scrum, we're talking about how to make the product development team effective. So as a facilitator, coach, and teacher, the Scrum Master's job is to enable the product development team to be effective at hitting its goals. They are an example of a leader, and their behaviours directly influence and will be copied by the team. Yet we are still seeing examples of Scrum Masters who assign work to the team, move story cards across the Kanban board on behalf of others, or manage meetings. None of these activities help the team become more effective and are not examples of leadership. What we need to have is someone who is more leading from behind, and by example. That means that the Scrum Master is a servant leader, which was discussed in Chapter 1.

## Product Owners

The Product Owner is another kind of servant leader; however, instead of serving the development team, they serve the organization to interpret customer and business needs into prioritized feature requests that focus on product development efforts. For the team to be effective, as already stated, we not only need the conditions for effective teams but we also need to have that one empowered, committed person whose chief responsibility is understanding the vision for the product and communicating the business priorities. The success of product development efforts is everyone's problem, and much of the team's success lies in the relationship between the team and the Product Owner.

The Product Owner is typically responsible for writing the requirements on the product backlog. However, this person may delegate some of that to people in the development team because the rest of the development team should know just as much about the product as the Product Owner in order to make tactical decisions on a day-to-day basis. The team needs to know as much as the Product Owner about the priorities and why. The Product Owner will prioritize features based on stakeholder expectations, based on the business case or a product vision statement. The Product Owner knows what's in and what's out of scope, and as a leader makes decisions and is accountable for the impact of those decisions. The person in this role is sometimes called the 'voice of the customer'.

Often this person will know tools and techniques like empathy mapping, creating personas, writing good user stories, and writing a product vision statement, to help bring the customer's view and the customer's needs to the development team. We have Roman Pichler to thank for collecting and creating these tools for the Agile development context. The collection of tools that can be found on his website (https://www.romanpichler.com) is aimed at creating a common understanding of the organization's customers, their needs, and the vision and purpose for a product development initiative. Agile Coaches using their 'teaching' skills will offer these to Product Owners and teams to help them work towards a common purpose. The choice of whether to use the tools is the Product Owner's and the teams. Even while teaching, we do not mandate tools, although we might mentor by offering a scenario in which these tools helped other teams, and how they were used in context.

As with the Scrum Master, Product Owners don't assign tasks to the team. We want people to stand on their own feet and think for themselves. The benefits of this are that the team owns all the decisions they make, owns the work, and ensures that the work is good quality. There's a sense of pride and ownership that we're all going to work together.

## Transparency, inspection, and adaptation

For me, the Scrum Events – Sprint, Sprint Planning, Daily Scrum, Sprint Review, Sprint Retrospective – help a team develop discipline to plan work for a short timeframe to a business goal, check progress and offer help to each other, review progress of the work done, and reflect on how to improve their processes. Discipline, say Katzenbach and Smith in *The Wisdom of Teams* (1993), is one of the factors that makes great teams.

Every event in Scrum except for the Sprint is a formal opportunity to inspect something and adapt something as a result. What gets inspected and adapted is one of the Artefacts. The Scrum Team, made up of the Development Team, Product Owner, and Scrum Master, plans only one Sprint at a time, so the Development Team's Sprint Backlog only contains, at most, one Sprint's worth of work at a time. And the work on a Sprint Backlog relates to the current Sprint Goal. Feedback loops are made explicit in almost every description of Scrum, but I recommend Gunther Verheyen's *Scrum: A Pocket Guide* (2013) and Esther Derby and Diana Larsen's *Agile Retrospectives* (2006) if you need to get up to speed with Scrum quickly if, say, the team you're coaching has selected Scrum as their starting point.

If the Sprint Backlog is the Development Team's place to manage its progress, the Product Backlog is the place for the Product Owner to track the team's progress in achieving business objectives, and for capturing changing business needs that get prioritized on a list of features that changes as often as the business and market environments change. The Product Owner's job is not to create the same old prescriptive plan of the past and assign that as a task to Development Team members, calling that plan a Product Backlog instead of a Gantt Chart. The Product Owner's key responsibility is to communicate the business vision and bring the high-level problems and opportunities to the team. The Development Team and Product Owner have collective responsibility for planning the work to be done in a Sprint.

In Scrum, a Product Increment is a complete piece of the complete product idea that meets the team's Definition of Done. It can be released immediately or held for release later. Ensuring that each increment of work delivered by the team is potentially releasable means that the team has included quality checking and defect-fixing into each Sprint. Whether or not an Agile team uses Scrum, or develops services instead of products, the concept of delivering small pieces of 'done' work has tremendous value and is at the heart of Agile frameworks. It comes from flow-based development with minimal waste: Lean.

Scrum's inspect-and-adapt cycles are continuous improvement cycles. Sprint Reviews are for learning more about what the 'customer' really needs, and to help build trust and gain acceptance of work as it is completed. Sprint Retrospectives are for the team to learn what to change in order to become more effective. Your solution-focused coaching skills will help greatly here in supporting the team to identify what it is doing well and to continue using its strengths, facilitate the agreement of a process for identifying strengths, as well as behaviours that help or hinder the team to work effectively. At a pinch, you could offer examples of strengths and behaviours that helped or hindered, as you observed them during the previous Sprint. The focus of all of the work during the Retrospective is how well the team achieved its Sprint Goals. Examples of things that typically arise from these meetings are the intent to seek better clarification from business stakeholders on the team's objectives and purpose, or software development practices that need to be changed, enhanced, or abandoned, or interpersonal issues. You will undoubtedly recall more topics from your work with teams.

I hear a certain sort of language about processes and tools from people at every level when I work with people to create agility in their organizations. Some of the biggest burning questions are: 'How do we know we're doing Scrum the right way?' and 'Which tool do you recommend for managing our work?'. You will have noticed from the previous chapter on mindset that 'individuals and interactions' are more important than 'processes and tools'. And we still use processes and tools quite a lot, but not at the expense of thinking for ourselves. I often wonder if people's enthusiasm for Jira, a work tracking tool is about team members wanting to have transparency of the work being done in the team, if the team selected it consciously after trying several approaches, or if the team was mandated to use it so that management could have a way to measure success by tracking task completion. If the reason for using Jira was the latter – and not selected consciously by the team to organize the work – then a big point about Agile teams has been missed.

I'd like instead to see teams and their managers shift the focus away from the 'correct' processes and tools to creating habit for reflection and feedback. The parts of Scrum that give us the ability to deliver value to the customer, are the inspect-and-adapt cycles created by Sprint Reviews and Retrospectives. They're used for soliciting and understanding feedback on what the team has just completed in the previous few weeks and then deciding what to do for the next few weeks; and reflecting on how to be a better team.

For example, a planning meeting uses feedback from the previous weeks to decide what should be delivered in the next iteration or Sprint, which is typically two to four weeks. If you say you're using Scrum and you're not asking for feedback and using it for forward planning, you're not using Scrum, and in fact not Agile. Let's take a look at two of the meetings in a little bit more detail.

Scrum's Reviews and Retrospectives, when done well, are the 'check' and 'act' steps of Edwards Deming's plan-do-check-act continuous improvement cycle. They're formal opportunities to learn what the product needs, what the team needs, and what the organization needs from the team.

To get the most value from Scrum, you really need to do your Sprint Reviews. The team must have a Sprint Review with business stakeholders, not just a Product Owner. This helps the team adapt the product requirements to get the work done in priority order. It helps business stakeholders understand what the team's working on, builds trust, and helps the team shift focus when, at the end of a Sprint – which is a few weeks long – they find out that actually the business priorities have changed and they need to do something slightly different. Skipping the Review is like putting the brakes on the opportunity to create business agility that our senior managers want because they have been reading about it in the trade press.

Also, to get the most value out of Scrum, do your Sprint Retrospectives. These can be a little bit uncomfortable, because in a Retrospective the team talks about which processes, techniques, and interactions among the team members are working or not. This is really where the hard work is. This helps the team adapt its processes and behaviours and mindset to be more effective.

I think if you want to really get inside Scrum, you should read 'The new new product development game' by Takeuchi and Nonaka (1986). They have been researchers and proponents of Lean management. Their article, in which they use a Scrum team in rugby as a metaphor for a whole product development team working together, inspired Sutherland and Schwaber to create Scrum. Along with Gunther Verheyen's description of the feedback loops and empirical nature of Scrum in his Pocket Guide, I was able to really understand Scrum at the level that Sutherland and Schwaber, and others, mean for us to use it. The Scrum Guide itself can be a little obtuse, but I like its sparseness. I think it forces us to think for ourselves. They refuse to give us prescriptive advice.

As the current favourite Agile method, I see a lot of teams trying Scrum and making a commitment to use it to get the benefits promised by being agile. I see a lot of poor implementations of Scrum too. I feel sad when clients tell me they threw away everything they did before – including processes and practices that were working for them – and replaced them with Scrum and Jira. Teams often want an accelerator to get started quickly but if the new processes and tools aren't adapted quickly, then independent thought leaves them and turns what should be challenging and creative work into drudgery. Why throw away practices that had been serving them well for many years? (I'm afraid the answer might be that some teams never questioned what had been working and why.) Scrum's skeleton-like framework insists that you add your own practices to the approximately seven working hours of sustainable working days, and insists that the team devise its own planning practices to fill Sprint Planning and re-planning during the Sprint. The comment I sometimes hear in response to presenting the intention of the Daily Scrum – that it's for the Development Team to find impediments before the impediments become visible outside the team – is 'How is the Scrum Master supposed to find out what's going on in the team if he doesn't go to the Daily Scrum?'. There's clearly some work for coaches to do to help the Scrum Master and Development Team strengthen their relationships with each other.

# DSDM

As a former project manager, my favourite of all of the Agile frameworks to teach, when I teach courses, is the Agile projects framework Dynamic Systems Development Method (DSDM). On the surface, it looks a lot like any other project management approach, with a process, principles, and roles. But get into the guidance on planning cadence and you'll see lots and lots of feedback loops.

DSDM's philosophy, that the 'best business value emerges when projects are aligned to clear business goals, deliver frequently and involve the collaboration of motivated and empowered people' (Agile Business Consortium 2017), encapsulates the focus and success factors of Agile projects.

DSDM has eight principles and five practices that emphasize empowered and engaged team members who have high business commitment at the team and project steering levels. It's fundamentally similar to Scrum in its use of timeboxes that contain all iterative development, and it contains heaps more guidance for people delivering projects, and not just product development teams that stay together delivering the same product indefinitely. This is the place for organizations to get a starting point for good governance of projects that allows for the inevitable change that could not be predicted, while developing products and services incrementally to demonstrate early proof of viability and return on investment.

Organizations that want to adapt their project planning practices to uncertain and changing environments will use an Agile approach that has very, very short planning horizons and allows them to commit to just a small amount of work at a time. Then they decide, based on what the business needs next in another short planning horizon (of weeks to months instead of months to years), what needs to happen next. By committing to a very small amount of work at a time, it allows the business to change direction without having this difficult, challenging conversation about what to do with work that has been started but not finished.

A critical part of DSDM is the concept of flexible scope. This is anathema to the traditional project management mindset of 'The client is going to get everything – now let's pad the estimates to make sure we get everything done!'. This is the bit that my course delegates have the toughest time getting their heads around, because as project managers and business analysts, they know it's what their project sponsors and programme directors are going to have the hardest time accepting.

When a project sponsor assembles their team to list requirements, they have more than likely selected people who know – and I mean really know – the business processes and systems affected by the change. And in my experience, those people are experts, and experts want to be as complete and precise as possible. So their requirements' lists have been known to be the biggest, most complete feature lists ever seen. Which of those features are expected to deliver the most value? That bit is a little murky, unless the project manager has a good business analyst with an Agile mindset to canvass business stakeholders and understand the market opportunity, intended customer segments, and probable business benefits over time. The agile mindset is that, some features will be more important than others, and will deliver business benefit earlier than others. The underlying assumption is that everything on the list will not be delivered at the same time, and if the business changes in the middle of a project, then some features will get bumped from the list in favour of others, or will be replaced by new, unforeseen feature requests.

The principle from the Manifesto 'The art of maximizing the work not done' is the most relevant to DSDM's idea of flexible scope. Less is more. Extra features are waste, because spending time, money, and people's commitment on delivering features that will be seldom used creates more to test and support over the product lifecycle. The challenge from a behavioural change perspective is this: we're proposing that Agile projects should not deliver all features on the requirements list, and should not start large batches of work that cannot be completed within four weeks from their commencement. But people like certainty, and often demand a detailed requirements list and schedule to show how everything is going to be delivered. How can you work with your coachees to be comfortable with uncertainty? Give them a technique for managing changing needs.

## Prioritization using MoSCoW

We know from the mindset explored via Lean and DevOps that we can't start everything at once ('big batch') and expect to deliver features quickly to customers. How do we decide what gets done first and next and so on? The MoSCoW technique and the Kano model are popular ways for teams to prioritize features for development. While it is not my intention to teach the techniques and processes of any of the Agile frameworks in this book, it is important to mention the distinguishing techniques that make the approach agile in mind-set. The key to DSDM is that projects have fixed time and cost, with flexible scope. This is anathema to the traditional or 'waterfall' approach, where it was assumed that the team would deliver the whole scope at the expense of meeting market demands (time), letting low-impact defects get into production (quality), and throwing additional resources, usually people, at the problem (cost).

**Must.** These deliver the most business value. The product or service won't work without this feature. The project sponsor will cancel the project if we can't deliver this. Legal requirements are a must. Safety requirements are a must.

**Should.** Also delivers business value but if we can't deliver it, we should find a workaround.

**Could.** Desirable but less important. 'Nice to have'.

**Won't have this time.** Now out of scope. Won't deliver in this iteration/release/project. (Agile Business Consortium)

## Does it need to be a project?

The overheads of starting up a team, allocating a budget, and providing project governance are not needed for in-house product development teams. A more effective approach is to keep the product development team intact and work in partnership with a business stakeholder to deliver value continuously. Further-more, I've noticed that all too often, a project manager who has no experience in the domain in which the team is working fills the role of liaison between the team and the business. Business analysts are often also asked to do this most unfortunate role, removing the possibility that the team can self-organize to create their detailed plan for how to meet the business outcomes.

If you question the usefulness of planning in environments that change frequently, consider reframing the purpose and value of planning. To me, the purpose of planning is to be able to examine, in hindsight, what turned out as you expected and what didn't. There are learning opportunities in making that a habit at regular intervals. Now I hope Agile project management practices don't sound too dissimilar to what Scrum Teams do in their Sprint Reviews.

## Project managers

I'm still regularly surprised when I hear people say, 'In Agile, we don't have project managers any more'. I'm disappointed at hearing 'Agile' used as an all-encompassing thing, but mostly that somehow people have got it into their heads that the people who have been managing schedules, onboarding resources, tracking spend and managing the budget, identifying risks and issues, and escalating things quickly, in order to keep projects on track, are no longer needed in organizations that deliver projects.

The motivation of team members comes from allowing them to take responsibility for how they design and deliver products, solutions, and services that the business needs. Empowerment comes from trusting team members to make decisions within their areas of authority. This is different to most project management frameworks that we might have come across, which shall remain nameless today, but we all know what they are: frameworks that tend to be very process-driven and heavy on traceability, documentation, and delivery of management products and artefacts. In Agile projects, we emphasize the motivation and empowerment of the team in order to deliver the right solution for the business in a timely way.

So why shouldn't we have a project manager to hold the budget and on-board resources, and manage risks and issues? I think this belief that there is no more need for a project manager is that there is no project management role in Scrum. Scrum is a product development framework, not a project management framework. Many organizations have successfully adapted their project governance and planning practices to bring in an iterative development and empirical planning style, which is very popular in Scrum and very effective when done well.

## Agile PM skills and behaviours

High-level Agile-style leadership for the team uses clear descriptions of the project goals, facilitation, and coaching conversations to support the team. The project manager coordinates at a high level and leaves the detailed planning of the actual delivery of the solution at the task level to the team. It's at this point that project managers who have been used to giving detailed instructions to the team ask themselves: 'So now I know what not to do, what do I actually do for an Agile team?'. We'll help you with that in 'Outcome-based planning' below.

Some more details are listed below about what an Agile project manager does in terms of their skills and behaviours, which is different to what usually comes to mind when we think of project managers:

- Agile project managers perform high-level project planning but not detailed planning inside Sprints or timeboxes.
- Agile project managers still manage risks and issues but in an agile way. They are highly available and visible to the team.
- Responsive handling of problems is escalated from the team in a management by exception way.
- Progress is monitored against the high-level plan – for example, a release plan, as they're called in Scrum or delivery plans.
- The project manager also motivates and ensures the empowerment of the teams to meet their objectives, and manages the working environment, including the physical locations of the teams, to ensure they have face-to-face communication as much as possible.
- Help and guidance are given to team members where difficult situations arise.

- Effective and timely communication is ensured, as is provision of information to the project governance board and stakeholders. Stakeholder management and good communication are thus huge parts of this person's role.

Now if we're coming from a command-and-control type of environment with project managers, and I used to be asked to do this as well as a project manager, we have to adapt. My manager said one day, 'Laura, you need to tell those people what to do.' I didn't know it at the time, but I just sensed there was something wrong with that. I knew that the architect and the senior consultant who were on my mixed team of external consultants and client resources knew more about what they needed to do than I did, and any attempts at assigning tasks would be met with a look of 'Who do you think you are?' Learning how to be more of a facilitative project manager, being available to run interference whenever there was anything that came up that could derail us, was what was needed, but it was different to how my job was described to me.

### Outcome-based planning

I'd like to give you an example of what I mean by outcome-based planning. The project managers separate the high-level view of the plan from the team's detailed view of the work that they deliver in very short planning horizons, e.g. Sprints. A project manager will typically have this outcome-based view, or high-level view, of the project and what needs to be delivered. The plan must describe business dates, release dates that are important to the business to meet business goals. Objectives of the planned releases should be able to be described in one very clear sentence.

For example, the objective of this release is to announce to the world that we sell books online. Release Two of this release is to communicate to the world what types of books are in our catalogue and which market segments we appeal to. In Release Three, the objective is to provide additional ways for people to order and pay for books online. It's very, very high level and does not at all get into the detailed work that the team needs to do, because the team members are the experts on how they can achieve the business goal, of a release.

The team's responsibility is in the details of each Sprint Backlog or Timebox Plan. The team's detailed plan of what they're going to deliver in a two- or four-week period is entirely the team's responsibility. We're still seeing a lot of Agile project managers assigning work or getting involved in how the team is working at the detailed level. This is one of the behaviours that we're working hard to change. You may find some discomfort in project managers moving towards this very hands-off way of working with the team.

How does the team know that what they're planning is the right thing? They always have that high-level plan managed by the project manager in order to relate the work that they need to do at the detailed level back to the objective statements at the high level. The implication for the project manager day to day is that they need to be looking ahead a few weeks and months with the 'sense and respond' skills mentioned throughout this book. Part of that is developing a network of peers to communicate the change taking place in the organization, find out what it means at the programme/portfolio level, and anticipate changes that could impact the project. To do this, the project manager must have their head up and out of the details. Leave the details to the people you hired for that work. Your inattention to details will allow the best people to do the product development work, and your improved relationships with team members will help you help them more effectively.

### Business analysts

Business analysts have some terrific skills with regard to properly analysing the business need and ensuring that there's proper communication for everyone to understand the proposed solution and to gain buy-in. I can therefore see the business analyst fitting into either the team leader or Scrum Master role, or even the Product Owner role, because the Product Owner often knows the most about the business need and can write very clear requirements to help the team.

A business analyst in an Agile environment therefore needs to really track change very carefully. I worked with great business analysts at the start of my career who were expected to appear at the start of a project with a list of thousands of detailed requirements and tell us, the project delivery team, that this is exactly what the customer wants. It's more important than ever now for the business analyst to remain engaged because the focus of the team can change from Sprint to Sprint as the business needs change due to changes in the external business environment (PESTLE). Agile business analysts facilitate teams to encourage creative problem-solving, critical thinking, and cross-functional understanding of business need and project purpose. Their big-picture view of the business and knowledge of the stakeholder environment makes them great candidates for the Scrum Master role, though they are seldom associated with that role.

# Manifesto for Agile Software Development

The Manifesto's four value statements and twelve principles indicate a mindset and behaviours which, the authors said, are required for teams to delight their customers.

The values and principles underpinning iterative software development were written down and were entitled the 'Manifesto for Agile Software Development'. Human factors, the authors said, were more important but do not replace traditional approaches to product development. The Manifesto is well-known and is mentioned in almost every book about Agile development. The values and principles have endured as the foundation and success factors for using all of the Agile frameworks – not all of which have endured to today, as the Manifesto has. The four values are:

## Four values

Individuals and interactions over processes and tools
Working software over comprehensive documentation
Customer collaboration over contract negotiation
Responding to change over following a plan

(Beck et al. 2001)

The core of the Manifesto is the four value statements. The 17 people who met in 2001 and wrote these down did something useful for us by making a comparison. Instead of just saying we value individuals and interactions, they're saying we value this over being driven by prescriptive processes and tools. A word of caution here – we're not saying we don't value processes and tools any more. We're saying that we used to put a premium on lots of detailed planning and design up front, believing a single best-practice process was a recipe for success. This is a hangover from the Taylorist management style that was prevalent during the First Industrial Revolution. The world has changed a lot since then and modern management practices recognize that Taylorism is dead (Pascale 1990).

We value working software over comprehensive documentation. Now you could call that 'working product' or 'working services', but it means the same thing. Again, this is an explicit move away from relying on lots of up-front planning that looks great on paper but doesn't flex with changing conditions in the internal and external business environment. We are categorically not saying that we don't write documentation any more. This is one of the most contested areas of the Manifesto in my courses on Agile development, and can be settled with this principle: consider who is going to read it, and when.

Customer collaboration over contract negotiation. Of course, we still have contracts, so we're saying that the relationship with the customer is more important than arguing over points in a contract. Create a relationship of trust that allows for openness in how you deal with the inevitable issues that come up during projects.

Responding to change over following a plan is perhaps my favourite, as a former project manager. The competitor landscape, regulatory environment, technology, suppliers, all will change regardless of what we've written into a plan. If you're running projects, plans are most useful for doing enough due diligence to know whether to start a project. That means plans start and stay high-level, and only become detailed for very short planning horizons such with Sprints in Scrum. This, in turn, reduces the risk that we'll commit to too much work at once and then have our best-laid plans scuppered by change that we didn't foresee or can't control.

The Agile Manifesto values, written in 2001, were given an update in 2016 by Darrell Rigby, Jeff Sutherland, and Hirotaka Takeuchi, in a *Harvard Business Review* article, 'Embracing Agile'. They made an explicit link to team learning.

The team learning behaviours in Table 2.1 may also require changes in behaviour of leaders if Agile transformation is to be successful. When leaders apply Agile values and principles in their organizations, they learn to 'speak the language of the teams they are empowering', 'experience common challenges and learn how to overcome them', and 'recognize and stop behaviours that

**Table 2.1**  Value statements of the Manifesto mapped to behaviours

| Value statements | Behaviours (Rigby et al. 2016) |
| --- | --- |
| Individuals and interactions over processes and tools | 'creative environment for problem-solving' and 'improve their work environment' |
| Working software over comprehensive documentation | 'learn faster', 'figure out fixes or move on', and 'experiment' |
| Customer collaboration over contract negotiation | 'specifications evolve', 'prototyping, frequent market tests', and 'constant collaboration' |
| Responding to change over following a plan | 'be happy to learn things that alter their direction' |

impede Agile teams' (Rigby et al. 2016). Studies on Agile teams confirmed the importance of communication skills, effective relationships, and team learning to success (Bermejo et al. 2014; Bierly et al. 2009).

### Twelve principles

While the four value statements are a high-level vision for how teams should work to get the benefits of agility, the twelve principles give more detail and bring them to life. After twenty years of working towards true collaboration and building self-awareness in teams, these won't come as a surprise to anyone who still hasn't read them. They are a helpful reminder and remain the baseline for Agile working practices. I've numbered them for ease of use but they're not numbered on the agilemanifesto.org website:

1  Our highest priority is to satisfy the customer through early and continuous delivery of valuable software.
2  Welcome changing requirements, even late in development. Agile processes harness change for the customer's competitive advantage.
3  Deliver working software frequently, from a couple of weeks to a couple of months, with a preference to the shorter timescale.
4  Business people and developers must work together daily throughout the project.
5  Build projects around motivated individuals. Give them the environment and support they need, and trust them to get the job done.
6  The most efficient and effective method of conveying information to and within a development team is face-to-face conversation.
7  Working software is the primary measure of progress.
8  Agile processes promote sustainable development. The sponsors, developers, and users should be able to maintain a constant pace indefinitely.
9  Continuous attention to technical excellence and good design enhances agility.

10 Simplicity – the art of maximizing the amount of work not done – is essential.

11 The best architectures, requirements, and designs emerge from self-organizing teams.

12 At regular intervals, the team reflects on how to become more effective, then tunes and adjusts its behaviour accordingly.

(Beck et al. 2001)

Principle 4, the relationship with the Product Owner, is one of the biggest success factors for Agile teams. In the original research I did in my dissertation, I found that the most successful implementations of Agile development were ones where there was a strong understanding of the business need in the development team. That comes from having a good relationship with the Product Owner who's empowered to make decisions. Principle 4 is therefore an enduring favourite of the twelve principles. A self-organized team is one that understands the business reason for the product development work they've undertaken, so that they can take ownership of how they build the product or solution without having to ask for permission when the tasks change. Principle 4 also challenges siloed working because to work together daily, I've seen the Product Owner eventually ask to move their desk to sit with the rest of their team – they now feel like part of the team. The organizational structure and culture merge when business people and developers work together daily.

To me 'the art of maximizing the work not done' has the Lean mindset all over it. Less is more. Keep it simple, get it done, defect free. Keep the design simple so it's easy to understand. Make it easy to test and don't overdevelop, don't throw in the bells and whistles. You may believe, hand on heart, that throwing in a little extra will have value – leave it out. Wait for an end-user to come back and tell you, 'I really did want that feature'. Now we have some tangible feedback or evidence that the feature is important to somebody. This is also an example of empiricism in Scrum.

Reflecting in order to adjust and tune behaviour is one of the skills that coaches should be bringing into all coaching, whether working with individuals or teams. The ability to see ourselves even a little by noticing our own emotions and reactions gives us the possibility of changing our interactions and breaking free of old habits. When the product development team does this, people are able to engage in sense-making at a level that potentially exceeds what individuals could do on their own.

## Introduction to timeboxing and the Agile principles

As a coach, you'll have been introduced to some reflective practice skills, so you know the importance of continuous learning. In my experience of teaching Agile frameworks such as Scrum, I've learned it's one thing to have facts, theory, and processes in mind, but quite another to engage in reflections and learning in a group. Here's a simple exercise I designed for my work with groups, and I've used it with success for years.

Set up an activity for your group to complete in a ten-minute timebox. Since Scrum's Sprints always have a goal, you'll suggest and agree a goal with the team. One that works well is to ask the team to describe the benefits of each of the twelve principles in a way that is highly visible. Note that this doesn't mean that the team should draw pictures. The purpose is to let anyone who comes into the team's room know what we mean by Agile mindset and behaviours, by using the twelve principles as a framework. I might suggest that the group uses some of the materials in the room, such as Post-it notes and flipchart paper. The point is to make the benefits visible if, for example, someone were to poke their head into the room. Could they see and read the benefits from the doorway?

You can thus see that the activity has a couple of purposes. One is to start to experience working in a self-organizing way towards a goal in a timebox, where you're in charge of how you organize yourselves and your work. The second one is as a learning activity to learn the principles. This is how we work in Scrum. As you go from Sprint to Sprint, you start to develop a kind of a rhythm of starting the clock with planning what you are going to do in that Sprint, based around a goal that is a business objective for the product, and then checking in with each other. Then you are prepared to demo, show and tell, and showcase the finished work to your business stakeholders, and you get into this rhythm of doing that on every Sprint.

Ask the group: What are some of the things that you noticed about the activity? What did you notice when we were working together? The group members might say things like, 'There were clear roles and responsibilities'. Ask them to think more by asking follow-up questions such as, 'Set by whom?'. Then follow up with, 'What were some more examples of that?'.

I make this up a little bit more every time I do it. Sometimes I change the quality criteria. Sometimes I make it fifteen minutes if there are more people than ten. I don't always ask people to group them into themes. Some of my groups will put things on the wall and everybody stands around the wall together and naturally starts to have that discussion. I might say that, 'I noticed that you didn't do that' and so I ask the additional question, 'How would you group these together into themes?' to get the individuals to discuss them as a group. Every group is different. Their meaning of the twelve principles is relevant to them, relevant to their context, and to the products and services that they build.

# DevOps

DevOps and the iterative and incremental approaches summarized under the 'Agile' banner have similar origins. In fact, one of the bedrocks of DevOps is continuous integration, which comes from the XP guys – who were well-represented at the meeting in Utah in 2001. The authors of the *DevOps Handbook* describe DevOps as 'the logical continuation of the Agile software journey that began in 2001' (Kim et al. 2016: 47).

For people moving to a DevOps culture, the easiest way to describe the mindset shift is that we are slicing through the over-engineered organizational structures that we created during the last few decades when we believed hierarchical structures would give us efficiency. Instead, we ensure that the people and resources we need to deliver on customer promises are available when we need them. This is very much the Lean mindset. DevOps takes forward the idea of prioritizing by only ever developing features that are important now. Small features are finished as close as possible to the time that development started. For me, DevOps resembles Lean and XP most closely. Continuous testing is a central tenet of Extreme Programming, and Lean's principles encourage us not to leave work on the shelf partially done.

As is the pattern throughout this chapter, I'm drawing attention most to the principles and some practices and tools of each Agile method. DevOps has The Three Ways, or principles of flow, feedback, and continual learning and experimentation.

## Flow

Create a fast flow of work through the whole value chain, from a concept for a product through implementation and operations. To make this happen, we make work visible, reduce batch sizes and work in short iterations, fix defects at the time we make them, and improve the process constantly.

The benefits of increasing flow are to respond quickly to customers' needs, improve quality, and reduce lead time – the time to move from concept to product launch. The practices that promote flow are continuous integration and, by extension, continuous build and deployment, limiting work in progress, scaling capacity, and running controlled experiments such as A/B testing.

## Feedback

Similar to autonomation, this is about empowering people to learn at the point of failure and put new knowledge back into improving processes. Part of learning at the point of failure is 'swarming', also called 'stop the line', as in the second pillar of Lean. It's an all-hands-on-deck issue resolution that lets a group learn together how to solve a problem and allows people to be where the problem occurs as quickly as possible. This last bit is the opposite to siloed working, in which interdependent people working on the same product pick up 'their piece' of development at a time that suits a scheduler, not at the time that people are needed. In Scrum terms, this is 'anyone needed to turn the Sprint Backlog into the latest increment' as members of the Development.

## Continual learning and experimentation

This is about creating systemic ways of using new knowledge, experimenting, and creating a high-trust culture to support risk-taking. Being generative – learning from experience and examining failures in order to increase organizational learning – replaces the counterproductive behaviour of hiding behind processes and contracts to weather organizational failures.

### Reflective questions

1  Think of a team that you have observed, or in which you were or are currently a member. How does the team express the values of XP, DevOps, and Scrum? What examples of your team members' behaviours can you point to as examples?
2  On a blank sheet of paper, draw the feedback loops of Lean, Kanban, Scrum, DSDM, and Extreme Programming. Where do the loops overlap, intersect, and adjoin?
3  What do the twelve principles mean to the team or individual you're coaching? Look for opportunities in your next meeting, coaching session, or Sprint Retrospective to link your coachees' behaviours to the twelve principles and four value statements.
4  How do Scrum's timeboxes turn reflection and learning into a habit?

# 3 The demands on business to adapt to change

**Why you should read this chapter**

- Agile frameworks were defined by software developers to better meet the expectations of our customers. What are the wider systemic challenges our customers are facing now?
- The reasons organizations make the investment to adopt Agile frameworks range from making a company look good to investors and buyers, to increasing their ability to get innovative products and services to market in a competitive landscape. What are the best business reasons for choosing to make the investment?

Business environments are increasingly complex and volatile, with two-thirds of respondents saying their sectors are characterized by rapid change (McKinsey & Company 2017). The problem, however, is that despite all of the earnest change initiatives and good intentions, many organizations are not achieving the benefits of Agile frameworks to release software and other products and services quickly, with better quality, and lower cost of ownership that results from well-designed software beating the competition to market. On my dozens of visits to organizations, delivering seminars and courses on Agile frameworks, and with the hundreds if not thousands of people I've met in the last two decades in my work as a consultant, coach, and trainer, the words culture, mindset, and acceptance of change are the ones that come up again and again as sticking points that restrict organizations from achieving the benefits. Everyone says that change is inevitable, but it seems that not everyone wants to accept that people are at the heart of change.

The world's largest global businesses are finding opportunities in this disruption, changing their products and services faster than ever before, and in some cases their entire business model. And those market-leading CEOs also recognize the need to develop, and even reshape, their own skills to take on the new challenges they face.

Much has been written about the so-called seismic shift we are experiencing in business. I'm referring to the ability of companies to get new product and service offerings to market quickly. Everyone knows it's here and everyone has noticed the change in pace for at least the last ten years, but many people are at a loss when it comes to: how to stay on top of what's current; how to anticipate what their business unit will need to do to meet the next targets; how to keep skills current for career progression; how to stop our phones from beeping constantly but to respond quickly to what is really important and how to tell the difference; how to claw back time in the day to finally work on strategic planning and developing the team.

Yes, we've heard that to solve today's business problems, which are characterized by complexity and therefore creative problem-solving, it takes a team. Business leaders at all levels are now being asked to shift their leadership style to put more trust in the team, but this seems to be at odds at times with our desire to know what's going on everywhere all the time, and to be the smartest person in the room. It's not only seismic shifts in technology platforms, but the style of working and organizational culture that needs to adapt to let us survive and thrive in a different world.

A number of factors are influencing organizations to adapt to change more quickly than twenty years ago. Technology platforms, globalization, the influence of social media, and free movement of people around the world are causing an acceleration of change at a pace faster than most of us could have foreseen. Even in the early 1990s, when most of the modern Agile frameworks were relatively new, the impact of a connected world was being felt thanks to the Internet and the flexibility of technology platforms that decoupled programmers from the physical hardware on which our applications were dependent. By 2001, a small group of leaders in software development gathered for a conference of sorts to discuss how they had adapted to a changing world. Little did they know at the time the impact they would have on the world of work.

Before the world adopted 'Agile' with a capital A as the umbrella term for the alternative processes to waterfall project management, we called them iterative and incremental (Larman 2004). The name Agile is not only incorrect grammatically, but it is not how the word was first used to describe the new iterative approaches. The Manifesto for Agile Software Development, written in 2001 by a group of leaders in iterative software development, describes four values and twelve principles for how to be successful at delighting business stakeholders and customers. It's about the so-called soft aspects of change, recognizing that communication, rapport, and relationships are the secret to success in software projects. While the name Agile as a noun seems to have become the brand for the way businesses cope with the pace of change, the work to improve the softer aspects of change are much harder to adopt than new processes and tools.

What started as a movement in software development has expanded into a full-blown revolution in mindset, leadership style, and new organizational culture. In 2017, the Scrum Guide – which remains stubbornly short and non-prescriptive despite Scrum's enormous popularity – made an important change in wording. For a document under twenty pages, which is the single reference for Scrum adopters, a few words mean a lot. Scrum was no longer just a framework for software development, and it is now officially recognized as a way for teams in all sort of industries, functions, and sectors to get focused work done In the final weeks before this book went into production, a new Scrum Guide was released.

While software development teams embraced the idea of less paperwork and more team spirit, businesses grabbed the promise of faster times-to-market. The cultural divide between tech and business hasn't gone away, and there are still two cultures represented by those two broad stakeholder groups that see 'agile development' differently and sometimes appear to have different motivations for using the processes. My motivation for writing this book is to show that although the language and culture of those two broad but different stakeholder groups may appear different on the surface, their aims are the same. To achieve what both tech and business want, a mindset shift and new skills are required. I believe that the mindset and skills must come from a coaching approach that empowers people to choose how they get their work done to achieve a goal, leading to stronger commitment to the process and outcomes and, as a by-product, greater job satisfaction for all.

# Sources of complexity and change

From the time I began writing this book, I started to compile examples of political, economic, social, technological, legal, and environmental change that impacts our organizations. This type of change is also known as disruption, disruptive innovation, globalization, global supply chains, and efficiencies brought about by new technology. This next phase of global know-how is often termed the Fourth Industrial Revolution (Thomas 2019). Influential management thinker Peter Drucker predicted this time would come when he described modern organizations as needing knowledge workers who delivered work using their experience, skills, knowledge, and creativity (Drucker 1999).

Table 3.1 is an attempt to collect examples of causes of change using the PESTLE model. Use your own notepad or any Post-it™ notes that you may have lying around to jot down more examples based on your own experience.

With so much change and disruptive innovation in progress and more yet to come, it becomes very difficult to stay on top of the new-new things in business. Your leadership coaching clients will face this daily and I would be surprised if a sense of exasperation doesn't get mentioned directly or indirectly by your clients who are responsible for delivering products and services in fast-moving markets. As Agile Coaches, we also need to be aware of what's happening in the world broadly so that, at the very least, empathy we show when a client discusses their job with us. Like so many of you, I've come to rely on podcasts as a great source of information about the many changes taking place all over the world.

The impact of Agile frameworks is being felt across organizations as complexity and uncertainty in business affects not only product and service development but most business functions too. As an example of this, in 2017, the Scrum Guide was updated to reflect ways that organizations are using Scrum to transform the ways they do product development and make business functions more efficient.

**Table 3.1** Sources of change and examples using the PESTLE model

| Sources of change | Examples |
| --- | --- |
| Political | UK Brexit |
| | Governments returning to territorialism |
| | Cybersecurity |
| Economic | Coronavirus – changes to production output due to quarantines and disruption to supply chains |
| | New trade agreements due to the UK leaving the European Union |
| Social | Inclusion |
| | Mental health |
| | Coronavirus – social distancing |
| | Black Lives Matter |
| | Income inequality |
| | Creating social value through new business models |
| | Social media |
| | Fintech's provision of new payment methods in the Third World, e.g. MPesa |
| Technological | Curbing the effects of the coronavirus by using mobile phones for contact tracing |
| | Bitcoin and blockchain |
| | Changes to supply chains due to AI |
| | Cybersecurity (see also Political) |
| | Cloud computing |
| | How we get news – social media platforms |
| | Workforce planning due to AI |
| | Fintech (see also Social) |
| | Robotics |
| | 3D printing |
| Legal | Workforce planning due to changes in IR35 implementation (UK) |
| | Adherence to climate agreements (see also Environmental) |
| Environmental | Compliance with climate agreements |
| | Compliance with corporate value statements |
| | Consumer products – packaging, cars |
| | Moves to use renewable energy |

Scrum has been used to develop software, hardware, embedded software, networks of interacting function, autonomous vehicles, schools, government, marketing, managing the operation of organizations and almost everything we use in our daily lives, as individuals and societies.

(Schwaber and Sutherland 2017)

Whether Agile, or Agile frameworks such as Scrum, are mentioned in name or are just references to iterative working that are used, the world of work has changed and it started in software development.

# Demands on people to adapt to change

This book is really about people, and the ways coaches help them thrive through change.

While organizations are adept at changing processes and implementing change programmes focused on the so-called 'hard aspects' of organizations, they have less competence in creating the behavioural change needed to embody the values and principles of the Agile Manifesto. Much of this book addresses the agile mindset and principles of the main Agile frameworks, but what's really being indicated is the behaviours of leaders and team members that indicate if we are agile or not. In *Managing on the Edge* (1990: 28), Richard Pascale writes that people believe a 'management mindset' is easy to spot; however, 'mindsets are more perceptual than tangible'. It is difficult to define and put our finger on whether we have it or we don't, as each of us sees the world through our own lens, which is coloured by our own experience. Evidence is easy to identify for products and services delivered on time, quality standards achieved, and a gain in new customers or market share, but a mindset shift and behavioural change are not so easy to measure.

## Leadership in the Fourth Industrial Revolution

If you thought that the examples of political, economic, social, technological, and environmental change earlier in this chapter seemed heavy on the technological dimensions, or if there seemed to be overlaps between technological change and the other aspects of PESTLE, that's because the impact of new technology is being felt across all sectors and industries. Technology-driven change is at the heart of what's being called the Fourth Industrial Revolution. This concerns not only the pace of change, as is often cited, but also the convergence of technology with other domains to create entirely new ways of working.

Writing for the World Economic Forum in 2019, the global CEO of KMPG, Bill Thomas, said one of the biggest challenges for leaders in the so-called Fourth Industrial Revolution – the accelerated business change brought about by new technologies – is to use data-driven analytics as well as intuition to make decisions. He says that many CEOs are still using intuition over data-driven analytics, but they must develop trust in the data and understand how it can be used in strategic and operational decisions (Thomas 2019). In 2018, of the 1,300 C-level executives surveyed, the ones who use data-driven approaches to business strategy were more prepared to take advantage of opportunities created by the Fourth Industrial Revolution (Renjen 2019). The implications for coaches working with these leaders is that we need to support them in learning new decision-making processes based on more than just intuition. Leaders need a combination of intuition and data to help reveal interrelatedness. There is no formula for becoming the next unicorn or navigating a business through the complex environments in which we operate now. Attention to seemingly non-rational ideas that come from intuition – a mash-up if you will, of disparate ideas coming from having curiosity and a desire to learn widely across disciplines – followed by testing these new ideas with evidence, is what is needed. When ignorance of data-driven insights is drowned out by our mental model, we need a coach to bring awareness to the evidence.

### Managing through uncertainty

BBC Radio 4's programme *The Bottom Line* made an attempt at addressing our inability to predict the future in the paradoxically titled programme 'Planning for uncertainty' (BBC 2019). Guests from Shell and Sungard discussed ways their organizations thought about the future and managed risks. Shell creates scenarios in the form of stories to play out what the future might look like. Sungard provides support for organizations to be prepared for any disruptors. As an IT company, Sungard started as provisioning IT infrastructure but now the company helps organizations with all kinds of resilience

Shell's process involves listening to everything an analyst says and looking for areas where areas disagree with each other. Then they create a story to imagine a new response to possible outcomes. The presenter asked the guests, 'What is uncertainty?'. Risk is one type of uncertainty but, Head of Scenarios Jeremy Bentham said he tries to think of uncertainty as a 'broad ground' in which a company operates, which opens up opportunities as well as challenges. He described uncertainty as a learning opportunity to 'manage opportunities as well as threats'. Sandra Bell, Head of Resilience Consulting at Sungard, said uncertainty provides opportunities for positive things to happen, as well as being exposed to risk. She said organizations must have robust and agile operations, thinking about 'what could catch us out'. Then she said that it's important to build a strong network and people relationships to build resilience. Finally, she said that leaders need to have situational awareness and good 'decision-making under stress with not enough information', which could be very difficult for leaders to do when they don't have all the information they'd like to have when making decisions.

# Links to Agile frameworks

For many people embracing Agile frameworks, adopting a new process is a starting point, but embracing the values and principles of the Manifesto are considered essential to increasing mastery of the chosen methods. Training courses on Agile frameworks continue to teach the values and principles of the Agile Manifesto and organizations continue to look for ways to become agile to cope with uncertainty in today's markets and maintain competitiveness.

Current mainstream management thinking is generally based on a mixture of cognitive psychology – which focuses on motivational goals and behaviour – together with scientific methods designed to map out and organize tasks, such as process engineering or project management. These disciplines do not leave much space for the possibility of complexity and unknowns (Cameron and Green 2015). In 1993, Peter Senge claimed we were in the middle of a mindset shift about management and the emergence of knowledge-based organizations. Two years later, Jeff Sutherland and Ken Schwaber presented the Scrum framework to the OOPSLA conference, formalizing the approach (Sutherland and Schwaber 2007). There has been a growing interest in applying complexity theory to organizational change since the 1990s (Grobman 2005). Complexity theory, and related theories from the physical science world, are being used to explain decades of failures in using linear, predictive approaches to deliver product development initiatives.

The most widely used Agile method today is Scrum (Version One 2017); the official reference for Scrum, the Scrum Guide, references empiricism and complexity science as established theory to support the practices espoused in the guide (Schwaber and Sutherland 2017). The article by Takeuchi and Nonaka (1986) is considered influential to the Scrum creators' thinking about the theory behind the framework, with Jeff Sutherland calling Takeuchi and Nonaka the Godfathers of Scrum (Sutherland and Schwaber 2007).

The creators of Scrum recognized that the markets that firms operated in, and the products they created, couldn't be predicted and planned through predictive approaches. The work from Nonaka and Takeuchi on: (1) how teams recognize learning (Nonaka and Takeuchi 1996); (2) from Stacey on the paradox of embracing unknowns in complex systems (Stacey 1996); and (3) from Senge on creating a learning culture in organizations (Senge 2006), are the theoretical backbone to Scrum (Sutherland and Schwaber 2007), and by extension the foundation of Agile frameworks, owing to Scrum's wide popularity.

Now, it is accepted as the norm that organizations are full of uncertainty and unpredictability. Modern management practices make the link between our inability to predict the future and the importance of an organization to develop the capacity to learn from failure. In the software world, Barry Boehm knew this as early as 1984, and described a model which describes the uncertainty that prevails in early stages of the product development lifecycle, when little hands-on work has been done on the product (Boehm 1984). Steve McConnell popularized the model over twenty years later, calling it the cone of uncertainty (Gryphon et al. 2006), although some studies challenge the cone-shaped reduction in uncertainty through knowledge gain, and assert that uncertainty remains constant throughout the development lifecycle (Little 2006). These early theories of how to be successful in software development projects laid the foundation for iterative and incremental software development, the precursor to Agile software development. Agile frameworks, while iterative at their core, add that human factors such as light leadership and collaborative team working are important to success (Larman 2004).

**Reflective questions**

1  How have your clients had to adapt their plans to change based on market trends? How did your coachees react to having to change?
2  Thinking of a time when you had to adapt your business or personal plans, what new habits or skills do you need to learn to manage through the change?

# Part 2

# Coaching Approaches

Part 2 moves us into the use of professional coaching for behavioural change in the context of organizations that seek agility. I have taken it for granted that readers know most of the coaching tools described that fall within behavioural coaching or goal-oriented coaching, which, Jonathan Passmore writes in the *Handbook of Coaching Psychology* (2007), seem to fit well with Western views of goal-setting, incentives, and reward of management in organizations. Other approaches in this chapter include solution-focused coaching, Gestalt, systems thinking, and neurolinguistic programming (NLP). Unless mentioned explicitly, the coaching tools can be traced to behavioural coaching.

If being a systems practitioner is about ways of being, engaging, and contextualizing (The Open University 2020), then my hope for this part of the book is to bring these to life through the Six Lenses in an Agile context scenario presented at the start of the book. Each of the subsequent chapters in this part focuses on one of the Six Lenses, using the associated part of the scenario for the lens. I'll expand on the scenario more before presenting the interventions that coaches can use for each Lens.

# 4    Lens 1 – Individual

**Why you should read this chapter**

- One-to-one coaching is often overlooked when engaging in Agile Coaching. Nevertheless, leaders at all levels benefit from coaching that acknowledges the personal impact of working in a constantly changing business environment.
- The responsibility is even greater for individuals to find ways to adapt to change and acknowledge that they can no longer be the type of manager who has the answers to all problems.

*I was asked to work with a business analyst to help him understand and address what the sponsor described as 'problems fitting into the team'. When meeting the business analyst, who I'll call Brian, I found him to be quite open to meeting me, because first and foremost he expressed interest in learning new things to expand his professional skills. His expressions, body language, and choice of words and intent expressed high emotional intelligence. This was clear to me from the first few minutes of meeting him. I felt clear at the time that this was not a case of a charm offensive, or telling me what I wanted to hear. This didn't seem to be the same person who had been described to me by the sponsor. Brian relayed to me some of his frustrations about his role as it was seen by others in the business unit, and he was eager for me to meet his line manager to help me understand a wider perspective on the issue.*

In the Introduction, I summarized the coaching competencies or stances required of Agile Coaches as professional coaching, mentoring, teaching, and facilitation, and explained my reasons to deep-dive into professional coaching as the most sustainable of the stances for helping leaders and teams achieve behavioural change. However, you may question my selection of some leader capabilities over others for this book, indicating a light mentoring stance mixed with professional coaching. My selection of leader capabilities is based on my experience of working in the sectors in which Agile frameworks are used most often, my experience of working in software development, and coaching leaders and teams that say they want to become agile. Lyssa Adkins writes in *Coaching Agile Teams* (2010) that, 'Agile Coaching carries agile mentorship with it'; however, I hold firm to the position that while these are areas that are likely to be relevant to coachees, the final decision must be made by your coachees. While it's useful to speak the coachee's and client's (sponsor's) language, and therefore you'll be familiar with the organization's typical business processes, resist your coachee's requests to tailor processes for them. I maintain that your client is best placed to decide what Agile done well means to them, and that 'good' will look different to each organization because each context, system, and culture are so specific to the organization.

At the time of writing this manuscript, we have experienced some of the toughest systemic problems ever: the climate crisis, the coronavirus pandemic, and inequality (racism, homophobia, and sexism), made visible by the Black Lives Matter movement. It's time for all of us to develop the ability to work with complexity for our own survival. In keeping with the choices I set out in this book, we'll look at the Six Lenses for seeing interrelationships in systems – which you as coach will need to raise awareness with your coachees – instead of presenting processes and tools. Relevant processes and tools exist, and if you're at a loose end, then may I direct you to *Systemic Team Coaching* (2018) by John Leary-Joyce and Hilary Lines, created with and largely based on the work of Peter Hawkins. The choice to organize the coaching tools in each Lens chapter recognizes the interdependence of Agile leadership and collaborative teams, and the wider stakeholder environment in which organizations work.

## Who gets coached?

When we think of project managers and business analysts, we often think of the team or people associated with the team. However, people in these roles are leaders too, because they are responsible for translating a business need into an actionable message for others. As a result, the way they interact with a product development team is important for modelling the Agile mindset and behaviours described earlier in this book. Project managers and business analysts I've worked with sometimes say they feel they're stuck between a rock and a hard place, because the behaviours their managers expect them to display are different to what Agile team members – who caught on to and embodied the Agile values and principles long ago – are expecting of them. Leaders at this level are not usually the subject of the best-selling leadership coaching books promoted today.

Agile leaders are found all over the organization and have influence on the mindset and behaviours in the organization to support agility. The following descriptions of leaders start with the people who are closest to the team. This is where, in the team, most of the creative and valuable work gets done to help organizations deliver valuable products and services. Thus the people closest to managing teams directly can arguably be seen to have the most influence. When we say influence, we mean influence on day-to-day interactions, collaboration, empowerment, and culture. Paradoxically, it seems that most books on leadership and management are written for senior leaders, executives, clients of executive coaching, C-suite, directors, and CEOs. Of course, the more junior leaders and managers learn leadership behaviours and culture from their seniors.

This part of the book discusses leadership capabilities that are important for leaders in fast-moving, competitive, uncertain business environments. I've organized them into six capabilities. For each capability, I've given a description and techniques from executive coaching that you can use to work with individuals. Note that this is not intended to be an exhaustive list of techniques that you can use with coachees. I have selected ones that you can use to support your coachee to enhance the capabilities for building agility.

# Critical thinking

Critical thinking involves rational thought, reflection, and evidence to increase knowledge and solve problems. It's important for leaders to be effective in the complex business environments in which we are working, said Helen Lee Bouygues of the Reboot Foundation, in an HBR Ideacast (2019a). Her work found that many organizational problems shared one root cause: a lack of critical thinking. She says critical thinking skills 'need to be learned and practised'. She says critical thinking is becoming harder with today's distractions and desire for quick answers. Ironically, the need to step back and reflect is more important now in the fast-changing competitive environments we are currently working in, rather than less.

Bouygues describes a three-step process for leaders:

1  Question assumptions
2  Reason through logic
3  Diversify thought.

Also, there are some things that leaders need to do to make room for critical thinking, such as taking time for yourself to stop and think – for example, going for a walk, managing emotions, or speaking to people who are in different fields.

Examples of where she's seen companies failing at critical thinking include: a pharmaceutical company that brought in a CFO who had little pure accounting experience. His 'biggest qualification' was that he was a good friend of the CEO. She said this is often evident in boards. This is an example of lack of 'diversity of thought'. For other leaders, 'blind optimism' and 'exuberance' blinds them to the ability to 'reason through logic'.

As coaches, we provide value by questioning and challenging our coachees' thinking and providing space for reflection.

### Decision-making processes

'When we are afraid, we try to become more secure', says ICF master coach Georgina Woodstra. The uncertainty in today's world has caused leaders to want to make things even more certain, leading to 'paralysis in decision-making'. She is noticing 'impetuous decision-making'.

Many psychological traps stop us from brainstorming and evaluating possible options before making a decision, for example the anchoring trap, in which we become attached to the first bit of information or solution that we see; the confirming evidence trap or confirmation bias in which we look for evidence to support a decision; and the overconfidence trap – especially prevalent in project management – in which we are overconfident in our ability to estimate and plan the future.

You can use this decision-making approach to facilitate a discussion of a business problem and generate options. The process helps leaders and teams avoid common psychological traps by using rational decision-making. The process is as follows:

1  Assess the situation
2  Define the critical issues
3  Specify the decision
4  Evaluate options and make the decision
5  Implement the decision
6  Monitor the decision and make adjustments as events unfold.

Though decision-making is presented here as being a linear and rational process, in practice decisions must be made with a balance of data-driven insights, rational process, and intuition. Intuition comes from so-called 'fast thinking', coined by the Nobel-prize winning researcher Daniel Kahneman (2011), in which we access knowledge quickly and, it seems, without knowing how. It's a shortcut whereby we have learned to access a lot of information quickly, which can help us in decision-making.

### Force field analysis

This is one of my favourites; I've used this with teams in many different contexts as a way to better understand a problem. The technique helps people see the factors that help or hinder the group in moving towards a goal.

The process:

1  State the goal, proposal, or problem.
2  List all of the forces supporting the change, and forces against, in the left and right columns.
3  Rate the strength of each force – for and against – on a scale; for example, 1 to 10.
4  Review and discuss the ratings for each factor.
5  Discuss ways to increase the forces supporting the goal and ways to decrease the forces hindering progress.

### Six Thinking Hats

This is also known as De Bono's Six Hats, as it was created by Edward De Bono. I am particularly fond of this approach, because as a coach I am often asking coachees to step into different ways of thinking, helping the whole group to see a goal, problem, or opportunity in new ways. Create some coaching questions in advance for each 'hat', which you can use to stimulate thinking by the people wearing the 'hat' in the meeting where you use the tool. I'm reluctant to offer questions of my own because I don't want to create the impression that magical thinking will take place if only you read the questions. Learn from what you're hearing from people during the meeting and create new questions on the spot to follow up and pick up on words used by your coachees to formulate new questions.

White hat: use the data available

Red hat: use intuition and emotion

Black hat: look at the negatives

Yellow hat: look at the positives

Green hat: use your creativity

Blue hat: process control

# Acceptance of 'not knowing'

The great paradox of working in the complex and uncertain environment in which we find ourselves is that there is more information than ever pushed to us but it is impossible to know exactly what the right path for our teams is. We need to be comfortable with not knowing answers and leaving behind our attachment to expertise. The good news is that when individual leaders don't know the answer, they can draw on the power of their team to do the hard work.

### Create a thinking environment

I recommend to the leaders who I coach to try Nancy Kline's approach to meetings, where everyone is heard and gets to speak. In 'Meeting This Way', in her influential book *Time to Think* (1999), Kline advises that the person chairing the meeting allows each person to speak in turn, asking them to 'say what is going well in their work, or in the group's work'. Each person is allowed to speak without interruption, and the chair or leader should ask open questions that ask for more information and clarity about statements that sound like assumption. Kline's 'Incisive Questions' provide a guide to doing this, but experienced coaches will know very well how to do this and can model it for a team. After each person has had a chance to speak, the chair should ask the group 'what went well in the meeting and what they respect in each other'.

# Resilience and adaptability

Carole Pemberton's book *Resilience: A Practical Guide for Coaches* (2015), describes the components of resilience in adults. She says that people in business gain resilience from personal traits, like a belief in oneself and optimism, a sense of protection such as having support, and what I think of as a 'stable platform' in personal and home life, plus the capacity to learn from experience. She says we also intentionally create conditions for fortifying ourselves with the capacity for resilience. She calls this a person's 'adaptive capacity'. It seems to have as much to do with ensuring our personal health and wellbeing is being looked after as consciously monitoring our thoughts and the helpfulness of thoughts in relation to the problem or situation in front of us. I see adaptability as the willingness to adapt to new external conditions, whereas resilience is a personal capacity to adapt when under stress. A better definition of resilience comes from Carole Pemberton: 'The capacity to remain flexible in our thoughts, feelings, and behaviours when faced by a life disruption, or extended periods of pressure, so that we emerge from difficulty stronger, wiser, and more able'. Central to resilience, she says, 'is the ability to remain adaptive when under strain and to re-orient to the new situation' (2015: 1). Anyone working in an environment with market pressures can recall easily the stress of a pressurized workplace when there's a lot at stake. Resilience and adaptability – which seem to follow close behind resilience – are essential for the frequent changes imposed on us.

Carole Pemberton's eight contributors to resilience and its loss, according to her evaluation of the research on resilience, are:

- Self-belief
- Elasticity
- Meaning and purpose
- Solution-finding
- Support
- Proactivity
- Emotional control
- Realistic positivity

Her resilience questionnaire in *Resilience: A Practical Guide for Coaches* is a useful tool for coaches and their clients to gain awareness of which of these are strong or weak.

### Adaptability in practice

Natalie Fratto is a venture investor. She presented at a TED Talk in 2019 about how she assesses start-up company founders. She wanted a way to identify the founders that would be successful. Some venture capitalists sort through candidates by finding out how smart they are – for example, where they went to university. But she says the 'single most determinate for me' is adaptability. She believes, though didn't provide any research on the topic, that adaptability is a form of intelligence. She describes this as 'AQ' or adaptability quotient.

She says this is important because of the amount of change we're experiencing: 'We know that the rate of technological change is accelerating. Each of us, as individuals, groups, corporations, and even governments, are being forced to grapple with more change than ever before in human history'.

Three ways in which she identifies people's ability to adapt to change are:

- Ask 'what if?' questions, such as 'What if your main revenue stream were to dry up overnight?'. Identify multiple versions of the future. Asking 'what if' asks people to simulate the process of imagining the future in different ways.
- Look for signs of un-learning. People who can 'un-learn' are challenging what they already know. We can change what we know through dedication and hard work.

### Re-write your narrative

Pemberton proposes narrative writing as a technique for helping your coachee build resilience, which she practised and studied as part of her doctoral thesis. By analysing the 'narrative' of her coachees, she identified that the loss of resilience was linked to 'a loss of identity that was key to their sense of self'. The identity that her coachees ascribed to themselves was destabilizing and blocked them from managing the challenge ahead. Your coaching work now is to support your coachee to create an alternative narrative, one that will support them in overcoming the source of the challenge to their resilience. For more about how people carry and develop a narrative, see Pemberton's work on 'The Narrative Wave' (Pemberton 2015: 43–44). It describes a pattern of moving towards a new narrative that is incremental, with small but regular steps back (which Pemberton calls 'breaks') from the narrative that a client might construct to explain their current position but which is not helping overcome their difficulty. The metaphor of the waves moving towards shore is a compelling way to help your coachee understand their return to resilience as a journey, rather than a one-time 'fix'.

### Solution-focused coaching

Solution-focused coaching, by virtue of its approach that looks at calling on past successes to build a way forward for the future, is a way for the coachee to draw on their own abilities to regain resilience. Solution-focused coaching reminds coachees of their successes and skills, which they can call upon now to move forward. As with all coaching, your coachee is responsible for identifying solutions. Encourage future-focused thinking by asking your coachee to imagine how they would like a situation to be in the future and how they have managed similar situations in the past; then identify the habits, techniques, or practices that led to success, which they could apply now. The focus on outcomes fits hand-in-glove with the outcomes focus of Agile frameworks. Don't be misled by the name 'solution focus' into thinking that you're providing solutions for your coachee. This is not teaching, or consulting disguised as coaching. For more on solution-focused coaching and all styles of coaching for behavioural change, an indispensable book is the *Handbook of*

*Coaching Psychology* (2007), edited by Stephen Palmer and Alison Whybrow. Its highlights include:

- Finding the exception to 'always' and 'never'
- Scaling
- The 4 Ss: Skills, Supports, Strategies, Sagacity – the words of wisdom, idiomatic sayings, and 'long-held truths' that motivate us.

### Miracle question

This is recommended by Pemberton as a technique from solution-focused coaching for helping your coachee find answers within themselves, based on their desired outcome. This is a well-known tool among coaches and is included here because of its broad applicability and relationship to solution-focused coaching. You should word the so-called miracle question in a way that feels natural and fits your coachee's context. The premise of it is that your coachee is now at a point in the future ('you've woken up tomorrow morning with the answer' is a typical case) at which they have the answer. Ask: 'What is the [answer]?'

### Achieving a sense of purpose

Pemberton says one of the ways that individuals can regain resilience when faced with difficult challenges is to find a sense of purpose in something. Relating our work and actions to a greater sense of purpose is highly motivational:

- What do I enjoy?
- What problems do I want to solve?
- What is on my 'bucket list'?
- What can I uniquely do or offer to be in service to others?

# Managing stress

This is another example of an area for coaching that could apply to people in any situation, no matter their job or complexity and uncertainty in their business environment. But for people at all levels in complex and uncertain environments, stress inhibits the future focus and rational decision-making ability that we need very much to manage through complexity. Here's some guidance for coaches to support your clients to manage stress. Understand your own sources of, and responses to, stress. Learning your own ability to manage stress well (or not) gives you greater awareness that will help you notice when your coachee is managing stress well (or not). Use your coaching skills to help your coachee take responsibility for their stress, instead of blaming it on others. Your coachee will need to address the cause of stress with others or manage things that are under their control. However, in either case your coachee must take responsibility for a solution. Fundamental management skills are important for managing time and expectations. Encourage a work/life balance to give your coachee perspective on the causes of stress.

In her book on resilience, Carole Pemberton says that when employees are asked to continue doing more with less, 'resilience can become stretched to the point where it cannot spring back. Elasticity becomes spent, and is replaced by a rigidity of thinking and behaving' (2015: 41).

Bringing mindfulness practice into coaching sessions, if you are trained in these practices, will help your coachee notice their thoughts and emotions.

---

### Box 4.1: Case Study: Adopting agile ways of working

Everyone wants solutions and everyone wants them now, but big organizations – public and private – often have entrenched approaches that can act as barriers to achieving real answers to challenges. Jason (not his real name), a solutions architect in a major public agency, has been leading a drive to get his teams and their members to embrace agility in the way they think and work. The systems that they have to use can be as agile as an oil tanker, though, and the attitudes of some senior management are more suited to being a captain of the *Exxon Valdez*.

'There's lots of good, up-to-the-minute cutting-edge work being done against very, very old back-end systems that are difficult to manipulate or move', he says. 'We're also having the same type of battles from a management point of view. We're kind of fighting people who don't get it and don't necessarily want to get it'.

People can get 'nervous' around Agile teams, he says. 'They see a lot of teams that are relatively junior, in their mid-twenties, doing very critical technical work and making those decisions to do that work and it makes people worried. It's a problem in the organization'.

Jason was once in the Army, when decision-making was a different process completely. 'I found out very early that on the battlefield it didn't matter what rank you were, if you had to make a decision you made it, you didn't wait for somebody else to come along. Software development is the same, you know, people have to make decisions in real time, and you've got to trust people, you've got to let them work'.

Different understandings of the concept of agility make it more difficult for the organization to absorb it into their practice. To a deputy director, agility can just mean pushing a team to work harder, which is not always feasible. Jason maintains that many senior civil servants have never operated in an agile environment, that their background is waterfall-based, so that when agile ways of working were being introduced their mindset was still that of waterfall, where outcomes are clearly set, whereas Agile is constantly cognisant of the fact that technology is ever-evolving.

'They're like, "Why did you pick to do it that way? And why have you stopped?" They're just not in that mind-frame of "things are going to change".

Whatever you asked me on Day One will probably be half dead in the water by Day Two because technology changes'.

Becoming agile entails culture change. To really keep abreast of changing technology, Jason says that teams and individuals have to be allowed to fail, simply because what was a good system one week becomes obsolete the next, therefore an agile structure allows teams to change practices and targets on the hoof so that they ultimately gain an outcome that is in everyone's best interests. To be allowed to achieve that means that the senior management have to trust their teams, something they are maybe not conditioned to do.

Culture is often difficult to change. Jason points to the example of Steve Jobs, who said, 'Why do we employ clever people and tell them what to do? We should be using these people to help build the right solution'.

Jason describes his working environment as resembling many other people's in that it is all fine and happy until a problem is encountered, and then they have to find a way round or over an obstacle. Agile practices were introduced to allow solution-finding to become part of the working process, but some mindsets are struggling to adapt. 'The question always comes up – "Why didn't you know this?" But it's a big organization, there's lots of technology, and not everyone is going to know everything, but it's how we react to it that makes it a success or a failure. Blaming someone else never goes well'.

'You need to keep people on your side – reliability engineers, security people, risk assessment people – keep a good relationship in place, so that when we have to go to them at the drop of a hat, to ask for something to change or to ask for advice, they'll help us'.

One of the objectives of Agile practices is to acknowledge that obstacles, problems, and failure are part of working life, and the big picture is served better by accepting this and looking for solutions rather than reverting to blame games. Jason wants to change this culture. 'We do a lot of cross teamwork with the other coaches and the other Scrum Masters in the building, to help them with an impartial eye. We tend to go in with an "Okay, what I can help you with? What are we trying to solve?" But from the management level, it's always "What have you done? Why have you done this?" There seems to be a blame thing there and I say to my guys all the time that if we got everything right 100 per cent of the time, we would know nothing, we would learn nothing'.

Transparency is another dimension that Jason asserts has to be factored into the culture of trust. Although he's finding that many management personnel are struggling to embrace new ways of working, he reports that some of them are opening their minds to the new realities. 'Senior management, they don't see it, they see success as that market indicator of how they're doing. But S—, he's more like the teams; he gets that if I tell you I want it on the first of November, if it's available on the 20th I'll be happy as long as you keep me informed. That's all I ask – keep me informed and tell the truth, and that's a key thing for us, especially at team level'.

'I always say to them – tell the truth and you've got nothing to remember. Start making things up and you've got lots of things to remember because you don't know what you said and you don't know who you said it to, so just tell the truth'.

Agile working aims to be many things – responsive, fluid, inclusive – but to achieve the goals it's designed to achieve, the right people have to be together in the room at the same time. Jason reports that a deputy director may get themselves embroiled in a technical conversation with an architect or a developer from another agency, but they – the director – may not necessarily be cognisant of what the technology is all about.

'When we go to any type of kick-off or discovery session with a customer, each of the leads should be at the meeting. We should have a lead developer there because he knows his infrastructure, he knows what these guys can do. The lead tester should be there because he needs to know things like, 'How do I fit into their testing program? How do they fit into mine?' The lead architect should be there to see 'if their brass fits with our infrastructure'. The lead developer should be there because he knows his developers, he knows their skillset.

'I never question my developers for why they've done something the way they've done it because they know how and why they've done it that way. I would never go up to them and say, 'You shouldn't be doing this'. I'd say, 'We hired you because of your skillset. I'm not going to now tell you that your skillset is not doing what it should be. You know if you're doing the right thing'.

'I have ten developers that work under me and we see more often than not that when they work as a team the velocity of their work skyrockets, that they work very, very well together. They're always passing information, always passing knowledge, and their knowledge is really good. When we dissipate them into teams with others, their work drops way off the scale because they're not thinking about the infrastructure in the estate, they're thinking about their team. Their work has been fantastic really, and quite underrated.

*However potentially game-changing an initiative or program is, or however great it is to work with, ultimately it's all about the benefit it will bring to the end user, which Jason affirms. 'I always say to my guys, "You've got to understand that somewhere along the line of what you're doing is a person that needs access to services and support in a timely manner"'. Referring to his organization's end customers, he says: 'You're actually working to help people who are not in a position to help themselves'.*

## Reflective questions for Lens 1

1  What did Jason in the case study mention as success factors for teams to deliver great services?
2  Who are the stakeholders in Jason's working environment who are important to his description of what success looks like in his organization?
3  How does a 'thinking environment' generate knowledge more effectively than relying on an 'expert' leader who provides solutions?
4  How can you start using critical thinking tools presented in this chapter?

# 5 Lens 2 – Interpersonal

**Why you should read this chapter**

- Healthy interpersonal relationships among team members are important building blocks for team collaboration.
- The way leaders relate to their teams can create or destroy motivation and empowerment.
- Good leadership practice has emphasized time and time again that if you want your team to be self-motivated, give the team more freedom to think for themselves.

*Lens Two – Interpersonal*

*I met with Brian and his manager, who I'll call Tanya, to discuss some of the feedback he'd received, and the stated reason for the coaching. (Note that Tanya was not the sponsor for the coaching engagement.) What I observed between Brian and Tanya was good rapport and a great deal of respect for Brian's position and quality of work by his manager, Tanya. Whatever impressions some people in the business unit had about an issue with Brian's interpersonal skills were not reflected in this relationship. Tanya described Brian's effort to change the way the business analyst role was viewed and showed support for his desire to improve 'the way things are done around here'.*

Often, the change your client seeks is generated from a foundation of interpersonal relationships that seem to say 'I hear you and respect you'. While some people coming from a technical background look for the most complex answers 'out there' to the problems they perceive, it is in these basics that a slow and steady stream of change takes place. Interpersonal relationships are, to me, the 'local' part of the often-used phrase 'think globally, act locally' that has proliferated thanks to the environmental movement. Interactions with colleagues are opportunities to practise and habituate the behaviours that we want to see amplified on a macro level. In terms of the Six Lenses model, that means that interpersonal relationships are foundational to the other Lenses.

# Facilitative leadership

One of the project manager's responsibilities, we said, was to facilitate meetings and have informal discussions with the team when problems arise. When the team makes decisions themselves about the evolving solution, it allows them to create more options to solve problems rather than taking direction and executing the decision made by a single person. Using Agile-style leadership – for example, coaching conversations rather than telling the team what to do or giving direction, using more open questions than giving solutions – encourages the team members to think for themselves, leading to greater commitment and buy-in to decisions that the team makes, and ultimately leading to greater quality of the work that the team is doing. When the project manager's high-level plan shows the business goals and drivers and key business dates, then the team understands why it's being asked to do the work, so that the team members can change and adapt the plan at the detailed level from Sprint to Sprint, as opposed to just delivering tasks blindly.

All of the Agile frameworks have regular touch points to help the team to be able to identify these interface gaps or issues while they're still small – before they become massive problems. For example, in Scrum we have a Daily Scrum, which is a fifteen-minute meeting held at the same time, in the same place, every day, assisting the team to be able to identify these issues. DSDM calls it a daily stand-up meeting, as does Extreme Programming. These meetings are for members to be able to discuss what's going well, what's not going well, in essence to ask each other: 'How can I help you today?'. Specifically, as a coach you'd expect to overhear things like, 'After our meeting, I can show you what I did on another project that was similar'; 'When I'm finished with what I need to do today, I'm happy to sit with you and we can put two heads together on that'; 'I know who you can ask about that – let's catch up after the meeting'.

Sometimes we find that teams in those daily meetings aren't having those open conversations. I have seen some evidence of different reasons for that, and often it comes down to leadership style. Often, when team members aren't really trusted and empowered to make decisions to achieve a goal for that short planning horizon – a two-week or four-week Sprint – then they feel afraid to step up and ask questions, and to openly describe problems that they're having. Things tend to be kept to themselves.

So when the leader demonstrates that issues happen, problems occur, and responds with 'I trust you to find the right solutions to the problems, but come to me when you're really stuck', then team members tend to talk about those things more openly. Leaders need to be conscious to show there is nothing more important to them than responding to requests for help. As a result, if a more hands-off approach is taken rather than a command-and-control position, the team is more motivated and empowered to handle issues quickly and own their solutions, knowing that when they have a serious problem they can ask for help. This is why a Scrum Master is a servant leader who helps to remove impediments that the team can't unblock themselves. You'll find the facilitative leadership approach described throughout the *Agile Project Management Handbook* (Agile Business Consortium 2017) and there are examples from research on teams (Edmondson 2012).

## Enhancing motivation

Helping an individual increase motivation also increases their commitment and drive to work towards a business outcome or team objective. Throughout this book, there are examples of how leaders help teams do the right work by focusing on outcomes instead of tasks. *Coaching Essentials*, a tools resource for coaches, offers twelve outcomes that affect a person's motivation. I've selected the ones that seem to be most important for Agile leaders and teams. I'm not saying that the others aren't important. The intention is to select the ones that stand out in the types of businesses that might choose to use Agile frameworks. Work with leaders to practise these outcomes, perhaps by role-playing them. The selection is as follows:

**Independence.** Ask, don't tell. Listen to what's being said. Help to create a link between a person's individual objectives and the organization's objectives.

**Recognition.** Provide positive recognition for what an employee does well, as well as raising things that need improvement. Provide opportunities for staff to participate in decisions that impact the wider organization, outside of the individual's direct areas of responsibility. In addition to increasing an individual's motivation, this has the important additional benefit of increasing the diversity of ideas raised for making decisions, leading to better decisions and information that a single leader cannot do on their own. I argue that this kind of participation is critical for complex and uncertain environments.

**Achievement.** Allow employees to set specific goals and solve their own problems with support from their own networks. Resist the temptation to jump in with advice – even if you think you know the answer. Allowing an individual to solve problems themselves and take ownership for work allows the person to develop a toolkit that will benefit them and the organization again and again and again. Giving answers disempowers people.

**Leisure time and pressure.** In highly pressured work environments with seemingly constant deadlines looming, it can be tempting for people to (metaphorically) lock themselves to the desk to get work done and not disappoint their colleagues and manager. Work with individuals to set incremental goals to stay on track, while encouraging a work/life balance to help staff manage stress, increase health and physical energy, and it will pay dividends back at the office.

## Inspiring trust

Work with your coachees to avoid wanting to seek and hold power over others. This is counterproductive to building trust and inhibits a leader's ability to be open to dissenting views. Why is this important? A leader cannot be everywhere all the time, and with so many moving parts and sources of change in organizations, they must rely on subordinates and peers to disagree with them and challenge their views. In her inspiring book *Mindset* (2006), Carol Dweck presents profiles of three leaders who had a learning mindset and avoided the power game that prevents leaders learning how to adapt.

Psychological safety – related to trust – is particularly crucial for organizations operating in complex and uncertain environments because it is precisely these organizations that need people to speak up so that the levels of input and diversity of ideas are as high as possible.

### Ladder of Inference

The Ladder of Inference, created by Rick Ross for *The Fifth Discipline Fieldbook* (Senge 2010), describes how our beliefs filter and shape our conclusions about the reasons for others' behaviour. The model itself describes the leaps in meaning that we make in the process of drawing conclusions, starting with observable, irrefutable behaviour:

* Observable 'data' and experience
* I select 'data' from what I observe
* I add meanings (cultural and personal)
* I make assumptions based on the meanings I added
* I draw conclusions
* I adopt beliefs about the world
* I take actions based on my beliefs.

(Senge 2010: 259)

Ross suggests learning how to test assumptions so that we short-circuit the leap to assumption that unfortunately could be wildly off the mark. This could be just as useful for Lenses 5 and 6 as for Lens 2. Here, the task for coaches is to support building new habits of testing assumptions by asking for confirmation of what has been heard and seen. This can be done as a summary statement, one of my favourite tools in coaching.

When you as the coach model this for others, it encourage the building of habits of doing this themselves, so that people get a fuller picture of what others mean by their words and body language. Even if your coachees believe that they understand the meaning of others' (verbal and non-verbal) communication, our maps of the world, which have grown from our own experience, get in the way of true understanding. Encourage your coachees to make space for asking 'checking' questions and listening openly to the responses they receive.

## Face-to-face communication

While Takeuchi and Nonaka, and Senge, made milestone contributions to understanding how individuals learn from experience, and the importance to modern management, Ralph Stacey brought a systems perspective, capitalizing on their work by saying that it is the ability of teams to experience working together that creates organizational knowledge. In effect, the individuals and their interactions, in a social context at work, are the mechanism for transferring individual tacit knowledge into organizational explicit knowledge (Stacey 2000).

For this learning and knowledge transfer to be communicated among one another, members of a system need to be in close proximity. This allows many small interconnected elements of the system to communicate values and other tacit knowledge about 'the way things are done around here'. Having roots in the physical sciences, organizations which are complex, with people who learn from the people nearest to them in the system, are referred to as complex adaptive systems (Olson and Eoyang 2001; Cameron and Green 2015). The characteristics of complex adaptive systems for knowledge teams, as described by Olson and Eoyang (2001), are the 'inability to predict the end state of the system reliably', and have self-organized structures of people that are 'more adaptive and more resilient' to change.

We therefore know that face-to-face communication is really important. Teams create knowledge using a shared vision and map of the organization and its customers, using social processes to turn tacit knowledge into recognized experience. However, we are finding that with the right skills and good facilitation, some teams are able to work remotely. That doesn't happen automatically just because they are using Zoom or some other type of video conferencing. Nevertheless, some teams are able to work really effectively remotely.

Where creativity is required, we need proximity to build on each other's ideas, and that means face-to-face communication. Where there's less complexity and more predictability – in other words, what we put in the plan actually came true – then we need less face-to-face. Then it's just a job of coordination.

In complex adaptive systems, where the products developed by teams are the result of knowledge work, teams learn what to do to meet project goals by working in close proximity and sharing tacit knowledge (Olson and Eoyang 2001). Advice from Katzenbach and Smith in *The Wisdom of Teams* (1993) is that to build trust and become effective, team members must spend time with each other.

Research on remote team working has shown that face-to-face, video conferencing, phone conferencing, and written communication show decreasing levels of synchronicity, thus reducing effectiveness in facilitating collaborative problem-solving and decision-making (Daft and Lengel 1986, cited in Andres 2013: 38).

Teams that develop innovative products need to work collaboratively to discuss options and trade-offs, make design decisions, and integrate parts of complex solutions; they find it difficult to do this when they are not physically located in the same place (Andres 2013: 38). When teams are working remotely, or virtually, meaning they are not co-located, the effect of not working face-to-face is that they do not continuously check that their behaviours support a common team goal on product development (Bierly et al. 2009).

Some literature disagrees with the industry literature with regard to face-to-face communication and small teams. Misra et al. (2009) reported on 'success factors' mentioned by their research participants and stated customer responsiveness as one of the highest rated success factors reported by research participants, as was the ability to get decisions made quickly, but reported team distribution and team size as low success factors.

# Considerations for remote working

Despite having the willingness and ability for many years to work remotely, it was undoubtedly the coronavirus pandemic and lockdowns of 2020 that accelerated our commitment to work remotely 100 per cent of the time. In our moment of need, remote working experts became busier while leaders and teams focused their attention on how, really, we work productively and with joy when we are all physically separate. We need guidance on how to adapt our behaviours to improve our leadership style, facilitation techniques, and group interactions to make virtual meetings work. Here are some of the issues that have arisen from the people I've worked with during the pandemic since March 2020:

- How do I make sure progress is being made on the project/launch/report/development?
- How can I have fewer of these meetings so I can get my real work done?
- I need exercise but I seem to be working more because I am doing childcare and/or home-schooling in addition to work, and that leaves less time for me to go for a run/walk/yoga before work.
- I have a repetitive strain injury from too much time at my laptop.
- It's taking longer to make decisions, or I'm not as involved as I used to be when decisions are made, or I was invited to the online meeting where the group was to make the decision but I couldn't get a word in/wasn't asked for my views/our boss made the decision for us.

## Learnings from Microsoft

Without a doubt, the move to 100 per cent remote working during the first lockdown imposed due to the coronavirus pandemic created learning opportunities for organizations, and many employees are reporting anecdotally that they love the new work/life balance. For others, being at home with children who need to be minded and reminded to attend classes from home, the boundaries between work and family have become blurred in an unsustainable way. Microsoft used the period to measure changes in the way employees of one 350-person business unit coped with 100 per cent remote working, based on application usage data. Here is what they learned (Singer-Velush et al. 2020).

Meetings got shorter – the number of thirty-minute meetings rose by 22 per cent and the number of meetings of one hour or more shrank by 11 per cent. People were tired of long meetings before the lockdown, and now questioned them openly. While meetings got shorter, work days lengthened by an average of four hours, and they believe the reason was to build time into the day for things like exercise and walking the dog.

Managers are on so-called 'collaboration calls' much more when working remotely, at the expense of time for 'focus and task work'. The Microsoft researchers measured this through time spent using Microsoft Teams. The managers who helped their direct reports the most saw their employees working less overtime: 'managers were buffering employees against the negative aspects of the change by helping them prioritize and protect their time'. However positive the short-term benefits were in strengthening relationships, the longer working hours for managers are not sustainable.

The periods of the day and night that employees are working has shifted, with meetings taking place at different times and even during the night-time. Work/life boundaries have changed, with some employees working three times as much during the lockdown as before. Encouragingly, people have found ways to maintain their social connections, and at Microsoft they increased the size of their networks. The article about Microsoft by Singer-Velush et al. (2020) did not measure the quality of social interactions or the benefits of building those wider networks.

## Lessons from Tes Engineering

The Tes Engineering team was created out of the understanding that no matter what your core business is, or what the needs of your customers are, every company is a software company. Tes describes itself as a digital education company (Tes 2020a) and operates an online learning platform and job-seeking network that was created from a more than 100-year-old heritage in the education sector. I spoke to David Morgantini, an early proponent of Remote First working at Tes, to try to understand the opportunities and challenges of mostly remote working as he conceived it before the coronavirus pandemic.

David says he was responsible for creating the Remote First approach at Tes Engineering initially (Tes 2020b). When he joined the London, UK office, he did it with an agreement that he wouldn't live in the UK permanently. 'I was hired at Tes as a contractor originally and I started working with one of the engineering teams. My contract was starting to come to an end and I also had a child on the way. Basically, we never had any intention to live in London, so we said we were going to just travel for the first year of my child's life. So I started travelling and it was great. I would be going to the beach in the morning and we're playing on the beach with my kid until I started working. Then you'd work for the day, then maybe take a long lunch break and then you go back and you finish your day and then it'd be later and bedtime and so on. I was able to spend quite a lot of time with my young child. It's something I recommend to people when they have this opportunity to be remote'.

That set a precedent for others to be able to work remotely, and eventually became a feature for new hires – supporting working styles that gave employees work/life balance. For example, one of their hires happened to be a keen trail runner who started with them in the South of England and then relocated to Edinburgh to be closer to the hills. [Appealing to the sense of adventure and freedom that I value in my own life, I was drawn to their Digital Nomad option in their blog, defined as: 'a London-based employee who has chosen to forego the comforts of London and the office and work from Wifi hotspots throughout the world' (Tes 2020a).] Remote working was further entrenched when Tes shut down their San Francisco office and told all employees that they could stay on, but working from home. One of the biggest benefits of Remote First working was being able to look for engineers in different regions of the world that may have a lower cost of living than the well-known tech hotspots, with their high cost.

Working with people in your team across distant time zones, for example, one with more than six hours' difference, can make collaboration difficult, but not impossible. David said it may not have been as effective as working in closer time zones. For example, the XP practice pair programming didn't work with people who were in distant time zones. 'If you're the only person awake, it's difficult for you to engage in those kinds of behaviours', he said. One approach that David and his colleagues settled on was to make sure that all members of a given team were in close time zones. They had organized themselves to allow for a more open-source style of work, which also allowed for distributed working and asynchronous coding practices. It was a nice coincidence that this remedied the challenge of remote working.

As David reflected on the evolution of Tes's Remote First work environment, he said it was an evolution, full of trial and error. It required a lot of small steps for the engineering teams to develop the culture over about a year and a half. Replicating their Remote First culture at Tes in his current organization, Class Dojo, would be desired, but he acknowledges that it's not possible to transform to go straight to what Tes created. Even though David knows 'what good looks like', Class Dojo has to go through the same incremental change as Tes in order to create their own remote engineering culture.

When I asked him what he would have done differently at Tes, knowing what he knows now, he said, 'I think part of the challenge is actually not so much what would I do differently. It's that I forgot the journey that it took to get to the place that I got to. I'm sure this is a challenge for a lot of Agile coaches – you've seen "good". You've seen the outcomes, you know what the right long-term goals are, and so you jump directly to them. But you forget that the journey to get there was actually a series of really small steps'. There is no blueprint, only evolutionary change.

### How I've made it work with coaching remotely

I stated earlier that creative, innovative work is best done face-to-face, particularly when a team is expected to produce results quickly. Remote meetings can be creative and spontaneous, although the physical distance reduces the opportunities to do this.

While many organizations have not made a 100 per cent remote commitment, all organizations we work with that have adopted Agile frameworks, or want to become Agile, will have messaging tools in addition to email and will have passed the learning curve long ago and know when it's productive and appropriate to use phone messaging, email, or pick up the phone. It's the in-person interactions that we argued used to require in-person workshops that are presenting the biggest challenge. But the tools are not to blame. If we're being honest with ourselves, many of our meetings were run haphazardly, or relied on luck to reach a decision.

The biggest learning from my experience has been this: everything is amplified in the online environment. When the facilitator designs opportunities for interaction, it pays dividends during the course. When little attention is paid to how to create engagement, it hurts even more online than if you were working with the group in person. If our interactions are amplified online, then we need skills to shape our interactions to get the outcomes we need from meetings. Many of you will already have great facilitation skills from your in-person events – the soft skills you use to engage and acknowledge people to make them feel part of your group. Your rapport-building soft skills are crucially important for ensuring that people feel they belong in the online group.

Outcome-based planning and team self-organization, which have been important to success with Agile frameworks and business agility, now become critical for letting teams get on and do the work. Data from Microsoft, shows managers increased their one-to-one time with direct reports during the start of the pandemic. That's not sustainable, and it ignores what we've known for decades about the power of teams – namely, that a high-functioning team can do more work and with greater quality and creativity than individuals can. Ask the leaders you work with: would you rather be the guy with a clipboard who walks around to each person in the team and asks, 'How's it going? How's it going? How's it going?', or would you rather make time to work at a strategic level, build relationships with stakeholders, and see results instead of completion of tasks?

### Create working agreements, aka ground rules or rules of engagement

All of your best facilitation skills come to the forefront here, and one of the first things an experienced facilitator does is agree 'how we are going to work together in this meeting/workshop/course'. Some of the statements that I find myself using with my groups again and again are:

- If you need to take a break at any time, to stretch, have a comfort break, attend to an urgent call, or get a coffee, just go do it. Please excuse yourself, and step out of the room (whether it's a virtual or physical room) and take care of your needs. No questions asked.
- Please respect whoever is speaking, even if you disagree with them. I want to hear from all of you, and won't miss you out. If you have a question and feel that the group is moving on, make a note of it on a Post-it. I'll be sure to pause and see what questions you have before moving on.

Mark Kirby mentions more ground rules and how he approaches safety in online meetings in 'Mastering remote meetings' (InfoQ 2019).

*Small groups for maximum learning*

Activities need to be scoped well for small groups, with transparent instructions that participants can refer back to. People may be working in breakout rooms and, unlike with in-person events, it's not possible to overhear people's tone of voice changing, which could indicate confusion or frustration with the work to be done. Give examples and set expectations clearly – and leave room for people to ask questions and clarify what they've heard – before sending people off to their breakout rooms.

*Get them to do the work*

For some group activities, roles don't need to be defined, in fact it's sometimes part of my instructional design to let the group decide how to get the work done.

For example, in my Agile Fundamentals module on Individuals and Interactions, one activity's purpose is to allow course participants to experience self-organization. For this type of activity, you need to be clear in your own mind about how much instruction you're going to give, and – contrary to the advice I gave earlier – allow the group to decide how it gets the work done. I offer participants the Lean Coffee approach, using any tools that they feel happy using.

Activities like self-facilitated Lean Coffee are sometimes chaotic, usually full of compromise, and require listening to each other to agree how to achieve the task together.

*Create psychological safety*

Activities are more impactful from a learning perspective when there is psychological safety. I've noticed the term 'psychological safety' being used a lot lately in the Agile community. I'd like to see it used, and understood, more for all learning events. And I hope that facilitators know that simply calling something safe doesn't create the safety.

I try to create psychological safety through intentional behaviours. You have just a few minutes at the start of the hosted session to show your participants if this is going to be another talk-a-thon by the coach/facilitator or an opportunity to contribute and be heard.

Encourage small talk at the start of the event so that everyone speaks as early as possible in the meeting. I became consciously aware from talking to Judy Rees about remote facilitation that the warming up and 'getting to know you' that happens over a coffee at in-person events isn't there for remote working. I had already made it a conscious practice to chat to my participants about the weather – literally – and about where in the country/world they are joining from, to get people to speak early and about something easy. 'Oh what's that picture behind you …? How's the weather in your part of the country …', etc., to be lightly curious about the person and show they're important. Now I make sure to plan time for coffee into the first ten to fifteen minutes of an online event.

Let people know, any which way you can, that you want to know what they think. Leave space for them to jot down ideas, take a screenshot of the slides and annotations in the meeting room, or use slides that present a single question for reflection. For example: 'What do these frameworks have in common?', 'How will my role change?', and 'What is a team?'. I like to use slides, but with extreme care, and tactically. For example, writing a thought-provoking open question in large text on a slide is a wide-open invitation to relate the session to participants' own experience. Get into the habit of asking open questions that stimulate thinking in order to encourage participants to relate the information you presented to their own role/work/life, even when working with groups or when the session is training and not coaching. Use all of your coaching skills in all online events, even if the event isn't labelled as coaching. People almost always have something important on their mind and they usually want to be heard. When they are heard, it helps other members of the group to learn too.

*Be aware of your physical space*

Make eye contact. I try hard to ensure that I can see every single participant's video all the time – not just the image of the active speaker. Then I drag the floating video palette left or right so that the image of the active speaker is directly underneath my camera – so that I have eye contact with the person as much as possible.

*Number of participants*

I know a lot of passionate facilitators and trainers who have a firm upper limit on the number of people for an event. I'm one of them. For online events, my preferred upper limit is eight participants, ten at a push. That's for my virtual Agile Fundamentals course using Zoom. There is no absolute number. What you can manage depends greatly on what is being presented (fifty participants is okay for webinars) or learned (ten at most with small-group work in breakout rooms), plus the comfort level of the facilitator with the tools and for managing groups generally. Experiment and decide what you're comfortable with. Don't be tempted to increase the number of participants. There is a tipping point which, when reached, means the quality of your online event collapses due to confusion and poor communication. I have experienced this with large groups in person. I don't ever want to find out what that limit is for online courses, as it's so difficult to get people re-engaged if you've lost them.

What I'll say about Google Docs or any of the other great collaborative tools like Lean Coffee Table, Trello, Miro, and so on, is that these are only really viable when everyone already knows how to use them. For some of my participants, it took a lot of courage to agree to do a course online instead of in person. Asking them to learn a new tool inside Zoom is a step too far for many people. When I facilitate online, I let the participants in each breakout room decide what tools they're going to use. There are a lot of benefits to letting the group decide, and as trainers of Agile development, we should be even more tuned into ways to empower a group and this is a great example of self-empowerment. So for my online events, I focus on making sure everyone can get into the

Zoom Meeting and then use all of the engagement approaches described here to make people feel part of the event. Then I draw on a suitcase of games, activities, and tools to offer to the group in-the-moment. When I'm stuck for ideas for energizing my group, I turn to Paul Z. Jackson's *58 ½ Ways to Improvise In Training* (2003).

### Self-awareness

As you can see, my own experience of capturing and retaining engagement online is essentially acute self-awareness and deliberate communication strategies, including tone of voice, while being myself. I don't always get it right – but the feedback I've had from my clients speaks to the effectiveness of my attention to communication online. Coaches must now work with leaders to gain self-awareness of what I call 'micro communication', so that what's seen and heard in a meeting is having the effect with their team that leaders intend.

### Self-care

Self-care is important for coaches and facilitators, as well as all of the participants in online meetings. Managing burnout, both physical and mental, is even more important when people are at their desks all day and teams seem to be 'always on'.

Kevin Doherty, who was responsible for online marketing for ICAgile, is a trusted colleague (my company, Future Focus Coaching, is an ICAgile Member Organization). In an email from him in the summer of 2020, after all of us had been working 100 per cent remote for several months, he said, 'We're all having to (re-)learn the importance of that kind of self-care'. That was in response to my message to him about taking a much-needed one-week beach and kayaking break in the middle of writing this book. When we're decades into our career, we think we've understood and mastered the work/life balance. But working 100 per cent remote has challenged that, so coaches need to go back to basics to ensure our coachees are looking after themselves. Since working 100 per cent remotely I have had to get a better desk chair, put more houseplants in my home office, and catch up over Zoom with colleagues and friends who I would have met 'after work' at a bar in London. For an extrovert like me, who gets energy from other people, those catch-ups are now critically important to my wellbeing.

But perhaps the most surprising thing, is that I have made the local park in my town centre an alternative working environment on sunny days, whereas for years it was just a patch of green that I walked through as quickly as possible, without stopping to notice anyone or anything, on my way to the shops. Changing the work environment from time to time is good for my mental health. I have had to make a commitment to going for regular walks in the middle of the day or whenever I have a break from meetings, or logging off early from work at 3 pm to go for a good cycle ride that energizes body and spirit. The old mindset of doing something naughty by leaving my desk at 3 pm is embedded in me and will take a long time to change.

## Box 5.1: Case Study: Making online meetings more meaningful

When a history of online meetings is written, 2020 will be the watershed year. From being a meeting option that some people favoured and some didn't, it became the *only* way to meet during the coronavirus crisis. Lockdown considerations aside, Judy Rees was asked to expound the efficacy of online meetings and training, as opposed to physical gatherings.

Judy's view of traditional webinars is less than flattering. First, she urges people to 'stretch their imaginations about what's possible online and stop thinking in terms of talk-over-slides webinars', then she drives her point home emphatically by stating, 'There's a reason you can't remember anything you've ever been told in talk-over-slides webinars: they're boring and they're ineffective as educational devices'.

If you make a living from selling talk-over-slides webinars, that would hurt, but Judy is insistent that for people to learn they not only need to have 'short, sharp chunks of information', they also need to discuss it with other people and see how others react, because people 'crowdsource their thinking'.

'When we're in conferences, when we're in workshops, when we're in training environments', she says, 'part of what we do is turn to the other person next to us and say, 'What did you make of all that?'

She continues, 'So the question is, how do we replicate those kinds of things when we're online? And the answer is you use some decent kits, set it up so that the relationships are human to human rather than human to machine'.

High-quality kit for Judy means Zoom, while she is withering about the 'Teams' platform offered by a very well-known software giant. 'I try to suspend my disbelief at just how awful this supposedly world-leading tool is for enabling conversations between people', she says. 'If you're lucky you can maybe see four of the people who are in the meeting. If you're the presenter and you share your screen, you cease to be able to see anybody. Presenters who can't see responses to what they're saying keep repeating themselves'. [Note: Since the interview for this case study, Microsoft has worked to increase the number of people who are visible at one time during a meeting; however, at publication the maximum number was nine (Microsoft 2020).]

One of the things that can be completely taken for granted when people convene in a room or a hall is that everyone is visible, everyone can seek out fellow attendees to talk to, or strike up a conversation with a stranger, but trying to replicate that sort of familiarity with an online group is very difficult. As Judy notes about in-room gatherings, 'The meeting probably starts when people go to the coffee area to get a drink of water. Then they walk together towards the meeting room, then they shuffle about with chairs and lights and paperwork, and together they set the space up. But when it's remote it's easy to imagine that as soon as you hit the button there's a group of people magically on Zoom, so you can start. But you've done none of the shuffling and there needs to be shuffling before people can settle'.

Judy combats that herself by setting up breakout groups, letting delegates familiarize themselves in groups of two or three, so that everybody says hello to somebody before the start. 'There needs to be a warm-up round of some sort as well', she says. 'I use a lot more warm-ups than I would do in room meetings, just to get people speaking into the space and realizing how it feels'.

Judy aims to make her meetings as inclusive of all participants as possible. 'I have my camera on permanent gallery view', she says. 'I accept that one of the downsides is that we're not going to have much eye contact, but as long as you can see each other, as long as you know that people are looking in the general area of the screen rather than off at their email or whatever, it's fine. People quite surprisingly live with changes to the way in which they normally interact'.

As well as aiming for as much inclusivity as possible, another interesting point that Judy makes is that meeting online increases diversity levels: 'One of the things we gain is potentially increased cultural and linguistic diversity, and diversity of all sorts, basically. Diversity is more diverse online than it is in the room'.

Judy expands this point by saying that on the day of this interview she'd spoken first with someone in Michigan, then with a colleague in the Netherlands, then with groups in Australia and New Zealand. 'We can have these conversations wherever we are in the world. You couldn't dream of doing that without this medium. I just think the medium has got enormous potential and we're not using the half of it'.

Another aspect of remote collaboration and working that is very important for some people is that it can be helpful for people who have less extrovert personalities. 'Personally, as an introvert, I find it much, much, much easier to find joy when doing this remotely than in the room. If I have to work with a group in the room for a whole day, by the end of it I am absolutely dead on my feet. Whereas if I do it online, as soon as I hit the button, you've all gone. I'm on my own, back in the office'.

Being part of a physical crowd can be very stressful for some people; Judy recalled a big conference that she'd recently been to where the organizers had created the contingency of escape tunnels. 'One of the stewards was a bit sensitive to crowds and he showed me that they have escape tunnels; he said that if you let the stewards know that you have sensitivities in that direction they say it's okay to use those spaces to get out, get quiet and chill before you go back in'. Despite the absence of physical gatherings of people at remote meetings, however, Judy says people can still struggle to cope with online working: 'People can be nervous and uncomfortable before they step into the space. They think that online events, online meetings, online training are going to be horrible. They've had lots of bad experiences in the past and it takes an effort of will to sit down and press the button to join. It would be nice if it were not so, but it is, so as hosts it's incumbent on us to make sure we're ready to welcome them into the space and make them as comfortable as possible, as quickly as possible'.

The antithesis to a comfortable online environment, though – in Judy's estimation – is a hybrid meeting. Hybrid meetings are Judy's bête noire and she pulls no punches in her disdain for them. 'They're universally horrible, awful, grim. There's a bunch of people in the room and some other people somewhere else. Most people's first experience of a remote meeting is that format, either being in the room and unable to hear the poor remote person, or, worst of all, their first experience is being the remote person and thinking

"I've got no idea what's going on in the room. They're all laughing, joking. I hope they're not laughing at me". It's a nightmare, it's absolutely not okay to put people through that'.

A participant in one of the meetings that she hosted has espoused Judy's view, to the extent that they said they were 'seeking out and destroying hybrid meetings wherever they could be found'!

Convinced that hybrid meetings are completely unfit for purpose, Judy started to scout for an appropriate symbol that would express perseverance in the quest to overcome tools that are unsuitable. The person who inspired her and has become something of a standard bearer for her is an Edwardian cyclist called Tessie Reynolds. 'Tessie Reynolds was the first woman to set a cycling record – from London to Brighton and back in 8 hours 38 minutes, in 1893. She was just sixteen years old'.

One thing she insisted on was the wearing of 'rational dress', rather than a long skirt that would get caught in her chain, and her determination has captured Judy's imagination. 'She said the minimum requirement to do this is shorts, fundamentally. She didn't wait until the birth of skin-tight Lycra suits and carbon frame cycles, she went for it. She ended up having her picture in a number of magazines; she'd made this clear choice – that the minimum she needed to get the job done was shorts.

*'I'm now Tessie Reynolds' biggest fan and I think that's how we need to be about the technology of remote meetings. We can't wait for artificial intelligence and virtual reality headsets, but we don't have to accept hybrid meetings and 'Teams'. We need to use decent kits so that the machine disappears and when the computer that's between us disappears and we can communicate directly, we forget that we haven't met the person in person.'*

---

**Reflective questions for Lens 2**

1   How does facilitative leadership enable others to perform better than command-and-control or other types of leadership? Think of people you've worked with in the past, and your own leadership style.
2   In what ways is building trust and rapport in online meetings similar to the ways we build trust and rapport in person?
3   Thinking about the good practice for remote meetings discussed by Judy Rees, what ways of meeting and collaborating have worked in your organization?
4   How do you know your work styles are effective for the work that needs to be done by your teams? What evidence do you have?

# 6 Lens 3 – Team tasks: Purpose and objectives

**Why you should read this chapter**

- Agile team practices are linked closely to good practice for team collaboration: for example, continuous learning and self-organization.
- The benefits of cross-functional teams include a behavioural element that goes beyond the availability of team members.

*Lens Three – Team tasks: Purpose and objectives*

*I had the opportunity to observe several teams' Sprint Planning meetings while working with this organization, including the team of which Brian was a member – before I was asked to meet with him one to one. As a product development team, the team members had a clear purpose (to build a software service that would perform a strategic business function of which they were all aware), and in this meeting they were focused on planning work for the current Sprint. However, there was no clear Sprint Goal defined that would allow team members to select items from the Product Backlog that they could use to achieve the Goal. Instead, I observed the project manager reading a list of items sequentially from a Product Backlog and asking for these next items to be assigned to team members, with an on-the-spot discussion of the technical tasks that individuals would need to complete in order to do the Product Backlog Items. I noticed a few anti-Agile behaviours and practices that would hinder any team, whatever processes they employed, Agile or not.*

- *The work for the Sprint did not have a stated relationship to business value because they had not defined a Sprint Goal at the start of Sprint Planning.*
- *There was no self-organization to discuss how the team would achieve the Sprint Goal. Tasks were assigned and individual names were recorded by the project manager somewhere.*
- *There was no collective ownership of the work due to not having a team plan (Sprint Backlog) that would be created and owned by the team.*

This is an all-too-common observation about teams. Many go through the motions of a new process without thinking about which practices are helping them achieve an objective. I prefer to think about the benefits of adopting a new framework, technique, or tools: 'What should we be able to do better or differently as a result of our investment in X?'. If you think learning and using Scrum is not an investment in business terms, think about the time lost and reduced completed work the team can produce while learning new skills. But on a behavioural change level, there was a need to address how the leader – in this case a project manager in a part of the business that was not part of my scope of work – understood the benefits of the process and tools and how to achieve those benefits. Working with the leader in this context would have been high on my list, but there are some great examples here of how the team organizes itself, which are addressed in this chapter.

The classic definition of teams is that of Jon Katzenbach and Douglas Smith: a team is 'a small number of people' who are 'committed to a common purpose' and 'hold themselves mutually accountable' (Katzenbach and Smith 1993: 111–120). This is in line with common Agile frameworks in which the team starts each iteration by creating a goal that every team member agrees to and works towards during the iteration (Schwaber and Sutherland 2017). Peter Hawkins (2017) adds that effective teams have 'effective meetings and internal communication', working 'individually and collectively' to engage stakeholders, with a team learning capacity to increase the capability of each of its members and the emotional health of the team in order to provide support and increase the commitment of team members.

Stability, a key idea of Bruce Tuckman's stages of group development towards high performance, is often cited as a prerequisite for high-performing teams. Today's product development teams are created and disbanded quickly, and we don't always have the luxury of stability in the environments in which there is a business case for Agile practices. This is even more of a reason, therefore, for coaches to help the team understand its purpose and establish at least initial ways of working quickly. It is equally important to intentionally establish cultural norms that create the behaviours for success across the organization, no matter the team structure of a given week or month. New team members will bring their own behavioural norms from their professional functional area, business unit, market sector, the organization, or national or religious culture, to their new team. In *Coaching the Team at Work* (2007), Clutterbuck cites some observations of teams that remained intact over a long period of time, which has potentially negative consequences. This contradicts the simplistic advice that high-performing teams are ones whose membership stays intact. The potential downsides of teams that stay together a long time are that they are less willing to change established norms which hinder them, they become less aware of the external business environment, and they have learned to 'bury relationship conflict' – or, as Argyris (2002) puts it, they are unconscious participants in organizational 'traps' – that become unconscious *modus operandi* for avoiding conflict and maintaining the status quo.

# Empowered decision-making

It should be obvious that effective decision-making by the team comes from self-organization. When the team makes its own decisions, its members are more likely to commit to the work. As coaches we need to look out for constructive dialogue and effective listening for discussing issues, generating options, and making decisions.

### Lean Coffee

Lean Coffee (leancoffee.org) is a democratic and team-led approach for deciding the agenda for a meeting and then having the discussion that the team voted on. The agenda and focus of the discussion are decided entirely by the team.

### Disney Creative Strategy

Created by Robert Dilts, based on an exercise that he heard was used at Disney in their creative-thinking sessions, Disney Creative Strategy is one of my favourite ways of brainstorming because it involves movement and a group working together as a unit, both of which generate energy for the work.

Choose three positions equidistant from each other around your room. You could invite participants to use a pad of Post-it™ notes with Sharpies for this, or any other method of recording ideas, but I like to tape an A1 sheet of flipchart paper to the wall. Something about the huge blank page encourages participants to fill it up – it's a joy to watch every time. Tape an A4 sheet of questions related to each of the three positions – Dreamer, Critic, Realist – next to one of the three A1 flipchart pages. Participants will use the questions to write about the product idea or business problem on their sheet. The questions are as follows:

#### Dreamer

- What do we want?
- What is the solution?
- How do we imagine the solution?
- What are the benefits of applying this solution?

#### Critic

- What could be wrong with the idea?
- What is missing?
- Why can't we apply it?
- What are the weaknesses in the plan?

#### Realist

- How can we apply this idea in reality?
- What is the action plan to apply the idea?

- What is the timeline to apply this idea?
- How can we evaluate the idea?

When I facilitate using Disney Creative Strategy, I like to invite participants to select one of the three positions I've set up around the room and write down as many answers to the questions as they can. Then I ask the groups to rotate around the room by one position, so that the Dreamers are now at the Critic position, Critics at Realist, etc. This allows the Dreamers to read what the Critics wrote and add to the flipchart their own ideas, which may or may not have been stimulated by the Critics' first pass of work.

# Learning capacity

In Chapter 2, we looked at the importance of experimenting and learning from failure. We saw that transparency in terms of problems and empowering workers to fix problems as close as possible to the time the problems occur is a principle of Lean. Amy Edmondson says psychological safety is needed for this to happen. This builds on work from Chris Argyris, Donald Schoen, Peter Senge, and many others in earlier decades, on the importance of creating a culture of learning. In Chapter 2, we saw the process implementation of a learning culture in Scrum's Sprint Review and Sprint Retrospective. In Chapter 3, we looked at the idea of a growth mindset in leaders, based on Carol Dweck's work, to be an example of a continuous learner, someone who does not have all the answers. Knowledge work requires learning from failure, and failures are raised when the organization has a culture of psychological safety.

The purpose of team learning in software development, or any product development effort, is for the team to reflect on which of its practices are helping or hindering, right now in the present. Each team is different, and the whole team is required to navigate the development process that's correct for the products it is developing, says Kent Beck in *Extreme Programming Explained* (2005): 'Each practice is an experiment in improving effectiveness, communication, confidence, and productivity'.

For product development, including software development, teams reflect in order to generate new knowledge that results in improved products, processes, and services. Duffield and Whitty (2015) created a lessons-learned model for project teams to learn from their environment. They point to research that calls for teams operating in complex environments to adapt their behaviour to be more effective in their own specific working environment. 'We've learned that organizations ignore team learning at their peril. In translating business ambitions into individual action, the support of team members and the explicit link to team learning goals are of fundamental importance' (Clutterbuck 2002: 67).

Research on effective teams outside the arena of Agile software development emphasizes the need for teams to learn to improve in complex environments (Clutterbuck 2002: 67). Clutterbuck refers to coaching as a way to support teams' learning in organizations. Research on supporting Agile teams to learn also sees coaching as a way to help teams learn by doing (Dikert et al. 2016).

My dissertation for the MSc in Coaching and Behavioural Change showed that when a team learns the organization's vision or strategy – the reasons why the organization needs the products under development – it can tailor its practices to be effective. The team achieves this by using customer feedback via committed Product Owners. The team may not have a detailed plan up front, and the usefulness of such detailed plans has been debated and doubted by practitioners (Boehm 1984; Gryphon et al. 2006; Little 2006: 48).

What type of failure is it? Not all failures should be embraced as a welcome learning opportunity. In *The Fearless Organization* (2019), Edmondson distinguishes among different types of failures, from ones that are the result of mindless mistakes in simple environments to trials that seek to test outcomes deliberately. The ones we're concerned with in companies that would seek to become agile – they are operating in environments with high uncertainty, competition, or innovating – are in her Complex and Intelligent Failures categories. She defines failures in complex environments as 'unique and novel combinations of events and actions that give rise to unwanted outcomes', and failures in intelligent environments as 'novel forays into new territory that lead to unwanted outcomes' (2019: table 7.2). Failures in complex environments are caused by 'complexity, variability, and novel factors imposed on familiar situations', and failures in intelligent environments are caused by 'uncertainty, experimentation, and risk taking' (ibid.). In other words, intelligent failures are required for innovation. Failures in complex environments represent most of the work being done in product development organizations.

### Building learning capacity with Action Learning Sets (ALS)

Not trendy or new, I recommend Facilitating Action Learning: A Practitioners Guide (2013) by Mike Pedler and Christine Abbot ALS groups are nevertheless highly effective and can be self-facilitated once participants learn the process for managing these sessions. They promote learning through reflection on participants' issues, which they select themselves.

# Cross-functional teams

Cross-functional teams create positive interdependence among team members to work together, with focus on a business problem or opportunity. Edmondson says when leaders encourage team members to be interdependent, it sends the message that team members must interact in order to understand how their work is interrelated.

Most Agile frameworks advocate a cross-functional team of three to nine people. You're going to see different numbers depending on which of the Agile frameworks you subscribe to primarily, and when you look at the advice for teams outside of the Agile pool, for example the Belbin team roles, you'll see a maximum of six people, which comes from their own research. You get the idea – we want relatively small teams. The team must also be cross-functional; in other words, everyone who is needed to design, build, and deliver the whole product is available all the time, for the whole product development lifecycle. All of these people are focused with purpose on the problems that are being solved, the customer needs being met, and the market opportunity that they're addressing.

Small teams that have skills relevant to the products to be developed, and helpful interactions between team members, are success factors for the use of Agile frameworks (Bermejo et al. 2014). Teams that develop products rely on members to have complementary skills (Katzenbach and Smith 1993). Some research describes Scrum teams that were ineffective because individuals prioritized their own goals ahead of those of the team (Moe et al. 2010). Co-located teams that are able to work in close proximity develop more quickly through Tuckman's stages of group development than distributed teams that don't see each other often. Proximity to each other helps communication a great deal (Gren et al. 2017).

In *Implementing Lean Software Development* (2007), Poppendieck and Poppendieck discuss the importance of designing products with operations in mind. A product lifecycle includes its operational use, and when product development is viewed in this way, the total cost of ownership of the product or service can be understood in full. I can't think that any business wouldn't care about the total cost of ownership. Nevertheless, many projects and product development initiatives consider only the cost of development. And worse, when the team and stakeholders have missed their launch date, they have one of those uncomfortable conversations about which lower-priority defects they can live with in the production environment, with a promise – which is rarely fulfilled – to fix those defects later. It looks almost farcical written down here; however, this happens all the time and I've had the unpleasant experience of managing projects that were forced to make the decision inevitably to accept the defects. When the cross-functional team includes people from operations, infrastructure, and security, for example, the team considers the total cost of ownership during the whole product design and development cycle. I remember with some irony a delegate on one of my Scrum courses who asked me if their relief manager is in the Scrum Team. Put aside for a moment your protests about having release managers and think of where a release manager, who would be responsible for ensuring that the team's product or service is fit for operations, would sit. They are part of the team, of course.

The development team is cross-functional. They are empowered and sometimes that's given and not just taken. Consequently, Scrum Masters and other leaders, other facilitative leaders, really need to make that space available for people to try things out without having to ask permission. People need to be self-organizing and knowledgeable. We tend to have expertise in a few products or programming languages or systems. This can be classed as T-shaped, meaning that we still have that expertise, the kind of vertical, deep knowledge and expertise, and then broad and shallow knowledge of everything else that the team is doing. That happens through close proximity when we're working face to face.

What about knowledge transfer? How can I do that most effectively for the whole team, not just one person at a time? People learn from each other, especially when we're in close proximity. So the members of a small, tight, self-organizing team will learn naturally from one another.

Creating cross-functional teams has clear benefits for relationships in teams, but organizations still put up resistance to creating them. Their traditional ways of organizing people – into functional silos – destroys the possibility to take advantage of the benefits. I'm often asked by my clients, 'can I still use Scrum (or DSDM) if we're not cross-functional?'. I typically respond to them with a question of my own: 'How agile can you be if your product development team members don't have the opportunity to build relationships and learn from each other?'. This way of working does cause change right across the organization. Expect discomfort – this is where change often happens.

### Box 6.1: Case Study: Evolution of an Agile team

If a runner is asked to run, they would expect the running track to be prepared. But it isn't always prepared. When Harriet (real name withheld) was asked to share her considerable experience of working with an Agile team that was looking to develop software solutions, she responded positively, looking to take up the challenge of bringing her new employers the benefits of Agile ways of working. Her brief was to deliver some Agile coaching and take on the role of Product Owner/Scrum Master, but this concerned her, given her new team's fledgling knowledge of Agile ways of working.

The organization that the team belonged to was extremely governance-centred, while the team itself was made up of 'bedroom' developers and contractors that had some experience of Agile, but the team itself was very experimental, and was considered as an exercise in finding out whether Agile practices would work for them or would fail utterly. Harriet's feelings about the team and her role were ambivalent at this point: 'There could be no doubt that the team had established a reputation for delivering business solutions that met customers' expectations and delivered significant benefit".

'However, the way in which the team was "organized"', she continued, 'although very loosely aligned to Agile principles in that it was self-organizing, was chaotic, with a team structure that could not be seen to be either waterfall or Agile'.

The Agile team was still an experiment, and the company culture was to a large extent at odds with Agile ways of working. 'The team possessed little or no business experience within the areas for which they were being asked to deliver software solutions and, in addition, the business users who were demanding solutions were not willing to release subject matter experts to work with the team. It was more controlled chaos rather than a team of people working in an Agile manner'.

Agile principles, in Harriet's estimation, are intended to flow through an organization, to rethink and re-model practices for everyone's benefit, but in this company, senior managers would often pull rank, demanding solutions if they thought their work was more urgent. In addition, solution requests were made through personal referrals; there was no control and the team itself was unbalanced, with analysis always taking precedence over solution testing.

Harriet responded by trying to implement some structure. 'Working with a contractor, we started to try and set up the framework that people in the team were happy to work with while receiving some Agile coaching from myself. We had one very significant advantage in our favour – all of the members of the team had respect for each other and the contribution that each brought to the team'.

The team was transformed into a Scrum team, where all the developers would work together on a single product or solution. Agile coaching sessions were conducted to explain and implement Scrum Meetings, Sprint Planning, Sprint Review, and Sprint Retrospectives, as well as establish the roles of the team members. The response wasn't as positive as Harriet would have wished, though. 'As the Scrum Master I was trying to establish the velocity of the team and, as we were all located in the same office area, discourage email and instant messaging in favour of getting up and taking to each other. This was strangely difficult'. Team members seemed to watch their own back a lot, which she interpreted as a lack of trust within the team; the organization still wanted everything to be documented, despite this being unnecessary, but the worst thing for Harriet was the lack of social interaction. They exhibited 'just plain laziness in not getting up to walk to the other side of the room to talk to a colleague'.

Under Harriet's mentorship, though, the team began to embrace Agile, but as the demand for their work grew, they needed more developers. This uncovered one of the major reasons for a lack of staff motivation. The packages offered to new developers by Human Resources were just not enough to attract high-quality staff.

'The inability to attract developers of the quality expected led the organization to consider the employment of contract staff', said Harriet. Unsurprisingly, the level of reward was too low to attract contract staff, so the organization could not recruit any new developers.

'Then the developers in post started to realize that they were under-rewarded for their work and took two courses of action. Firstly, they started to refuse work that did not improve their experience and, secondly, they started to dictate which Apps would proceed and when'.

Mutiny! 'In effect, the organization now had a development team that were running the department with no reference to the Product Owner or Scrum Master', explained Harriet. 'The most senior developer now ran the team and decided on the work to be undertaken'.

Part of the problem was that the Human Resources Department would not embrace Agile frameworks and therefore treated the team like the rest of the organization. The developers dominated the rest of the Agile team, demoralizing the other members, and the management was reluctant to intervene in case the developers all left and software production ended.

'Respect and trust died', Harriet sighed. 'Individual egos abounded and a pleasant and constructive environment to work in became a bullring of competing priorities'.

While it is rare in modern business for workers to behave like descendants of the crew from *HMS Bounty*, this example highlights the fact that for Agile approaches to work, the whole organization has to buy into the idea. 'Although people in the Agile team should not be seen as "better" than people in other IT areas', said Harriet, 'Human Resources need to realize that reward is based on the availability of skills. People with rare skills will attract a higher reward package'.

*To rescue the experiment and try and implement Agile more effectively, Harriet had to take a step back and re-scale the team. She brought in junior team members who were keen to learn and tried to get rid of practices and processes that adversely affected the team. Most importantly, she has used her coaching expertise to educate supporting departments in the business to understand and embrace the challenges, rewards, and benefits that Agile offers.*

### Reflective questions for Lens 3

1 Thinking about the case study, which of the Six Lenses did Harriet describe in her attention to the team's success? What additional stakeholders should Harriet invite to participate in the team's inquiry into how to succeed with Agile frameworks? Recall the Six Lenses and the example in the Introduction.

2 Thinking of a team that you coached, what has helped or hindered the team to be self-organizing and empowered, build learning capacity, and work with colleagues across functional lines?

3 Reflect on your own beliefs about continuous learning and a learning mindset.

# 7 Lens 4 – Team relationships

**Why you should read this chapter**

- Team relationships require special attention to enable collaboration, yet many organizations overlook the relevant factors.
- Psychological safety is now considered a prerequisite for high-performing teams. We know how to create it, yet it is quick to erode when management becomes stressed and reverts to command-and-control behaviours.
- Much has been written about how to build resilience. This chapter presents practical tools to support your coachees.

*Lens Four – Team relationships*

*My impression of Brian's work with the team during one Sprint Planning meeting was as a facilitative member of the team who proactively sought clarification from team members, attempted to summarize what he heard, and make sense of the implications of what he heard, greatly benefiting everyone else in the team. It is important to mention that the team was split across two geographic locations and met over a teleconference, and some team members spoke English as a second language. In this type of environment, miscommunications tend to be more frequent than when team members are co-located. Perhaps unknowingly, Brian fulfilled the facilitative role of an Agile business analyst extremely well to help the team better understand the business problems and features under discussion. The team's project manager/Scrum Master was running the meeting by working down a list of tasks that she assigned to the team for the Sprint. In this type of environment, miscommunications tend to be more frequent than when team members are co-located. Personally and privately, I questioned the strength of the relationships among team members if so much communication was mediated by the business analyst and the project manager.*

Coaching that supports team members to strengthen relationships can be the hardest type of coaching with Agile teams, but it also pays the most dividends. It is easy for misunderstandings to take hold and cause a team of committed and talented individuals to achieve not much more than a task list, as I described in the scenario. The goal for the coach here is to support the team to design their own ways of working and not 'structuring, facilitating, organizing, and telling the team how to be better', says ICF master coach Georgina Woudstra (2020). '[B]ehavioural coaching interventions that address issues such as coordination of activity, communication around specific tasks, or managing conflict that disrupts essential collaboration are likely to have a positive effect on performance', says David Clutterbuck (2007).

Group maturity is an important factor in whether groups build the capacity to learn and grow. In a review of the academic literature, (Fontana et al. 2014) reports that mature Agile teams share knowledge and continuously improve their practices, as well as address group dynamics that may hinder the team's performance. To improve the team's practices, an organization must address conflicts in the group and create opportunities for the team to become better by challenging them with different product development ideas and supporting their development (Gren et al. 2017). Gren and co-workers' study links behavioural change to agile transformations: 'transitioning to agile teams is closely tied to developing the team from a "group dynamics" perspective, meaning the [research participants] define the main challenge as the behavioural one ...' (2017: 115).

# Trust and psychological safety

The words psychological safety are used to describe meetings or environments where you're likely to feel welcome and your ideas valued. But to me, I know psychological safety when I see it, or rather when I feel it, and a label isn't necessary. It's present when you feel you can speak up and challenge the most senior person in the room, when you can present ideas that seem to 'go against the grain', or feel like you're the only one talking about the elephant in the room – without fear of negative consequences. It can feel scary when you're challenging your team, because all of us humans want very much to be accepted by the group. Belonging in groups is a feature of our evolution and there's no way around it. So it can be difficult to speak up when we think or feel we might be the only one who sees things differently. And yet one of the most powerful features of teams is their ability to see more problems, opportunities, options, and solutions than individuals can. To harness this benefit of teams, we need to hear each other out, to listen and build on each other's ideas. Psychological safety underpins the success of teams.

Amy Edmondson writes in *The Fearless Organization* (2019) that psychological safety is the foundation stone that enables all other success factors for teams. Her research on groups and teams at work reveals the interdependencies among people who do 'knowledge work'. 'The fearless organization is one in which interpersonal fear is minimized so that team and organizational performance can be maximized in a knowledge-intensive world. It is not one devoid of anxiety about the future!' (Edmondson 2012). She describes the benefits to organizations of having psychological safety as better collaboration, sharing innovative ideas, and learning from mistakes. She cites a study at Google

(Duhigg 2016) that examined the success factors for their best teams. Of the five factors the study identified, psychological safety was the basis for achieving all of the others.

The importance of trust shows up in DevOps where Gene Kim and his colleagues describe the importance of a 'high-trust, collaborative culture, where people are rewarded for taking risks' (2016: 34). He goes further to say that failures are planned in order to build resilience, mainly in the context of system failures and system resilience. To me the choice of words is uncannily similar to how we hope to develop Agile teams too. The reason for trust and safety in teams echoes the reasons that Edmondson gives in her book on psychological safety, namely that psychological safety is a prerequisite for learning.

## How to create safety

Edmondson dislikes the way the term 'psychological safety' is often used because it evokes a 'sense of cosiness'. And what it really means is 'candour', 'taking risks', and being 'willing to ask for help when you're in over your head'. In other words, it's about how people work together when things are tough, things go wrong, and we make mistakes. Edmondson says it's rare to have psychological safety, and therefore it should be a competitive advantage for companies. She says people want to 'look good'. So people tend not to want to say risky things.

Edmondson believes that an industry that's very difficult to succeed in is the movie industry. Pixar had 17 consecutive blockbuster movies, which she attributes to a co-founder and leader who has 'gone out of his way' to create an environment where 'candour' and 'critical feedback' are expected. She attributes this to two facets of an organization:

- Behavioural: a leader will say 'here's a mistake I made', which shows humility.
- Structural: setting up sessions to make it easier to give candid feedback.

In creating a fearless organization, three activities for leaders are:

- Setting the stage: What's the nature of the work and the project? How much uncertainty do we face? How much interdependence?
- Inviting engagement: Be proactive in asking questions to find out what your people are seeing/hearing/experiencing.
- Responding productively: A great response to a problem is, 'Thank you for that clear line of sight', not getting angry. Each of us is allowed to make mistakes.

### Challenge mental models

In addition to the Ladder of Inference, a well-known approach for challenging mental models that may be unhelpful comes from Chris Argyris, who for decades studied and developed our knowledge of how organizations learn. This approach for challenging mental models was described by Senge in *The Fifth Discipline* (2006). At a workshop Senge attended, he watched Argyris ask everyone present to recall a conflict with a client, colleague, or family member, then recall what was said, what was not said, and what everyone was thinking. The stories revealed how our beliefs were created to protect us from something that is no longer important in the present and is not helping us.

### Defusing tensions

It's almost inevitable that, at some point, tensions will develop during normal work and a leader will need to manage an emotional outburst. Use this approach to work with your leader to manage those situations well. A simple approach for handling people when they burst with emotion is *acknowledge-ask-answer*.

For some people, the first step may be to pay attention to their own emotions, recognizing how they feel as a result of the colleague's outburst, to name and contain it. Admittedly, this is easier said than done when faced with someone who has confronted you with a strong emotion, but like most things it takes practice:

- Acknowledge what you're hearing, feeling, and seeing about the person.
- Ask questions to understand more about the meaning behind the person's words.
- Answer the person's questions and concerns as best you can, or agree a way forward to get the person's issue or concerns addressed.

### Wise Crowds

Wise Crowds from Liberating Structures is useful for tapping into as many diverse viewpoints as possible. *The Surprising Power of Liberating Structures* (Lipmanowicz and McCandless 2013) is, along with *The Fifth Discipline Fieldbook* (Senge 2010), a treasure-trove of facilitated activities for a group to expand its thinking quickly. Like all of the Liberating Structures activities, the group or team is in charge and its direction is not 'led' by a so-called expert. The activities are deeply empowering and put group members in charge, which results in better-quality outcomes and increased buy-in to decisions. In the spirit of *Shu-ha-ri*, try them, tailor them, and make them your own.

Wise Crowds will have several uses for you, and I find it useful where discussing things in a single large group may sometimes produce stress or dissension, which hinders its progress. The authors of the approach, Henri Lipmanowicz and Keith McCandless, recommend organizing a group into small learning groups of four or five people each. In practice you could use larger or smaller groups – I've used a version of this with groups of eight to ten people. If you want people to be able to speak and be heard more, set up the activity using smaller groups.

In each learning group, participants take it in turns to be the 'client' or a 'consultant'. When the client speaks, they describe a challenge and ask for help.

When I've used this in learning groups with coaches, the 'client' in the scenario may not even ask explicitly for help – they may simply describe a problem or something that needs attending to. Ensure that each group manages to adhere to strict time-keeping, so that everyone gets the same amount of time as a 'client' and as a 'consultant' in each client round. After a client has had a chance to present a topic or issue, members of the 'consultant' team in the group should ask clarifying questions, then offer advice. Sometimes asking clarifying questions is so powerful that no advice is needed.

# Creating resilience in the team

In *Coaching the Team at Work* (2007), Clutterbuck proposes a version of scaling in solution-focused coaching for use with teams. Similar to the use of solution-focused coaching as a way to help individuals build resilience, his use of scaling can be used to help teams build resilience. Adapted to the product development team context, you can use the scaling technique to ask the team how well they met the Sprint Goal on a scale of 1–10, with 10 representing perfection in reaching the Goal. After asking the team to identify a number on a scale, use some of the following questions – or create some of your own – to follow up:

* What was your biggest contribution to help the team reach the Goal? (based on Clutterbuck)
* What surprised you about how the team reached the Goal?
* What did you do that was unplanned?
* What would the other teams advise you to do to improve?

As if any reminder is necessary, always ask open questions from the position of understanding more, so that you model this kind of open inquiry for others. Agreements such as 'no blame, don't interrupt, ask a follow-up question to gain more understanding' are helpful. Default to asking the team what agreements they want, and create a habit of revisiting those agreements every time the team meets for its Retrospective.

---

**Box 7.1: Case Study: Empowering the team**

'You can't argue with success' is a maxim beloved by businesses who don't see the need to change a winning formula, but it can quickly become a millstone around their neck that drags them to their doom. The speed with which the British shipbuilding industry shrank from making over 50 per cent of the world's ships to less than 2 per cents is a vivid illustration of this, so when David Taylor, Head of Special Projects, was asked to introduce a way of working that ripped up the rulebook at the long-established engineering company

Rolls-Royce, the challenge was not only to get management on board but to get his team to buy into the idea.

Rolls-Royce is a world-renowned engineering giant that is synonymous with quality, but like any modern business – or probably any business that's ever traded – it faces change. 'We have a lot of challenges within our business', says David, 'which have driven a different mindset to accelerate projects that we had previously been doing that needed to be delivered faster, and at a scale that we'd not done before'.

David's area of responsibility is delivering support to the company's Services business, but the way in which that support has to be delivered has changed: it has to be faster and it has to be more reactive. 'We have a very long cycle business', he explains. 'We use the waterfall method – you design, then you validate, then you deliver an end product into service. That approach is the one that we are most familiar with in business, and the one in which most of our complex programs run'.

In reaction to Service challenges, the team ripped up the rulebook. David set his team a target to deliver a radical solution for a tenth of the cost and in 10 per cent of the normal time. 'Previous experience said it would normally take about fifteen months to deliver this sort of program, but we set the challenge to deliver it in fifty days. We had to completely change how we designed and delivered that solution by using a different approach'.

David handpicked a team that he thought was up to the challenge. He brought them together in a different environment, away from their normal offices and surroundings and distractions, and explained their remit. 'The way in which we framed it was, "Don't tell us whether you can do it or not, tell us how you can do it"'.

The start wasn't easy, as he explains: 'After the first day, the team said there was no solution. At the end of Day Two, a similar story, they said "It can't be done". And one of the guys had the courage to stand up and say why it was going to take fifteen months. After a bit of a pause somebody else said, "Okay, so we'll do it like this". Then they set a new idea that we'd never done before'.

The project that the team was tasked with was designing new tooling to complete remote maintenance for their engines. David says that these would normally be a bespoke product. 'The solution they actually came up with was to change from a bespoke furniture mindset to more like "Ikea meets Meccano" – where you bolt things together and make things in a much simpler way. A focus on simplicity enables you to think differently in the way you design and the way you manufacture'.

The freedom to think differently kick-started the team and inspired them to meet David's challenge of seeing *how* they could achieve the goal rather than *if* they could achieve it. David's coaching role at the start of the project was not to direct them through it but to ask questions, not to provide answers. In the first few days they asked for help, but by the end of the second week they stopped asking. 'They knew that they were empowered', says David, 'and we saw an inspirational output from them. They picked it up and their energy levels just went through the roof'.

Once the team had bought into the vision, the next step was to bring the senior management on board. 'We brought the senior sponsors to the launch session', says David. 'On Day One they knew what we were doing, the context and the goal. They knew we were trying to deliver an audacious goal'.

The normal way of working would have been to present a plan within a governance framework based on previous experience, but David sold the project in such a way that an Agile approach was adopted. 'The senior leaders came to see the team. They understood the context. My role was to isolate the team from the normal process and make sure that our seniors would give it the right support, which they did. In doing it, you just saw the team thrive and you saw them take real ownership of the task and innovate to achieve the goal. It helped the senior leadership to realize that this approach could be scaled'.

A lot of external inspiration was sought in support of these projects. 'The example we used at the time was Space X, how they had done their rockets. They delivered their satellite launches with a cost of about a tenth of what the previous NASA launches cost. We named the project based on that *External Inspiration*. From then on, all of our projects had a name and the team used the names to create a level of identity'.

This theme of external examples was developed with a second project called *Project Bannister*. It was so named, he says, 'because the project they set out was so challenging that prior experience said it couldn't be done, which was a bit like the four-minute mile. Some people said it was not possible, but after it was done, five weeks after it, people started to break the same record'.

Not everyone in the business supported the projects initially. David dealt with this by being completely transparent, copying the key stakeholders in on everything so that they could see the regular outputs. By the end of the first project they had begun to be won over. 'And interestingly', he enthuses, 'one or two of the people who were initially quite sceptical have become the biggest supporters of it'.

Although David emphasizes that the team were given the freedom to achieve their goals without having to report back to governance committees, his influence in helping the team to achieve was still there. He exhorted them to step back at times, to look at their project from a distance and think big (think 10× not 10 per cent), to 'just take one step back, for a short period of time'. He encouraged them to look at how they'd delivered with the different ways of working, and how this style could be brought back into the business. 'It might sound counter-intuitive', he says, 'but you need to take some people out of the business for a very short period of time in order to go faster'.

David's influence with the wider business increased at this point. 'We worked with some Agile coaches within our business and we pulled a simple training exercise together where this success story was used as an example that has a level of application across the business'.

Rolls-Royce is a worldwide business and seeks to operate in a global context. For David that means working with teams outside the UK, and both he and the company welcome diversity and different ways of working. On a more recent project his team have been working with a team in India, holding a video conference every morning to 'set the drum beat of what the team need to do', in David's words.

'This is not a governance meeting as such, it's about helping more and judging less: "What help do we need?" "How can we do this?" And it's worked', he says. 'The team have found a cadence, a daily cadence, which I think is the important thing'.

Prior to this cross-continent collaboration, David went to India and met the team face to face. 'We really set the energy level and excitement around a goal', he explains, 'in a way in which we got the whole team engaged. The Indian team brought diversity of thought that was empowering. They were given a blank sheet of paper to help us think differently, and from that, the project really took off'.

Originally, they were two completely independent teams, never having formally worked together, but David wanted to 'connect the dots', although he was aware of the challenges of trying to do that remotely within a Scrum framework. Despite that, the diversity of their approach brought opportunity: 'Their experiences were very different. And the way in which they solved this problem was very different to how we'd have looked at it in isolation'.

*Setting, as David puts it, the 'audacious goal' is very important because it has changed his own approach as well as those he coaches, from a scenario where teams work within a set framework to one where, as the coach, he assists rather than instructs. 'That has been the biggest learning curve for me – that this is not a traditional project team leader approach, you need a coach to get things going and help keep it going, within a different structure. It has been great to see the energy of teams develop. For teams who want to get training or coaching, I will sit and answer questions to help them think differently, as a team'. The use of an Agile framework coupled with audacious goals has led to some transformational projects though some inspirational teams.*

### Reflective questions for Lens 4

1 Thinking of a team that you have coached, in what ways has a lack of psychological safety hindered the team in speaking up?
2 List as many facilitation techniques as you can that you have used personally in designing processes for meetings. How did each help or hinder the team to become self-empowered and make decisions as a group? How do you know the group was empowered or disempowered?
3 Thinking about a team you coached, recall the group's commitment to their output from the workshop, the quality of the dialogue, who contributed to the dialogue, and your own feelings about the group's work and process.
4 List as many success factors of using Agile development as you can, based on the case study of David Taylor's work at Rolls-Royce. If successful transformations include values, behaviour, and organizational process (Pascale 1990: 67), then can you group the success factors by values, behaviours, and organizational process?

# 8    Lens 5 – Stakeholder interfaces

**Why you should read this chapter**

- Traditional definitions of team coaching ignore the stakeholders that influence the team, as well as the systems in which the team works.
- To be effective at product development efforts that require buy-in and support from outside the immediate team, the team and team leader need to work with the stakeholder environment.

*Lens Five – Stakeholder interfaces*

*Brian described differences in other people's view of his role, specifically that the purpose of a business analyst was seen by his department as being different to his view of what was needed from the role to support the team. He described a sense that others did not value his contributions as much as they should have. Through informal conversations, I learned that the staff reporting lines were quite separate among the project managers, business analysts, and technical roles such as testers, developers, and architects. Each entity seemed to be working to different organizational objectives, and indeed I discovered later that the measures that each group worked to were different.*

*Observation of the team's project manager showed a command-and-control leadership style, task-level management, and driving the conversation with the team instead of Agile-style facilitative leadership. This indicated that the business unit favoured a management style that was focused on the delivery of tasks instead of outcomes. My observation about the project manager correlated to what I had learned and observed about the business analyst through our conversations, and in his interactions with the rest of the team.*

So often, working in organizations, we are loaded down with the immediate tasks-at-hand. We forget to pick up our heads from the work to see how we relate to others. The reminders to use active listening and ask questions, display genuine warmth, act with integrity, and to be calm and assertive, are crucial for working in organizations.

# Focus on a single product

Have you ever been on a project where it was kind of running into trouble and going off the rails? I knew the answer to that was going to be 'yes'. Did management ever put in place something where they said we've hired out a conference room for the next six months and we're going to protect the six of you and let you focus on this and get it done and do it any which way you can? That's what we mean when we say an Agile development team is focused and has 'all the skills as a team needed to create a product Increment' (Schwaber and Sutherland 2017). It's about eliminating distractions and letting people focus on getting the job done. This reduces the wastes 'delays' and 'handoffs' defined in Lean.

When we have 'James', now assigned to three different teams, three different projects, or the same team but three different things around the organization, it's very difficult to get anything done. It decreases our ability to predict when we're going to be able to deliver that product because it exponentially increases the complexity in the working environment. The main thing is to get the team to focus on one thing at a time. This has been problematic in a lot of big organizations as well. We have all these things to do. How else are we going to get them done except to ask James to work on three things at once? Well, it means that all three of those things are now going to take longer. And in the meantime, longer initiatives are more exposed to change in the internal and external business environments. So focusing on one initiative at a time also means understanding business priorities in new ways, and making each project as short as possible so you can finish one before something causes you to change direction.

# Customer focus

One of the challenges that we're often finding is that the Product Owner, who is meant to be a representative of the business requirements and the voice of the customer, is not a real representative. This person is perhaps appointed or reluctantly asked to be the Product Owner to the team, when they perhaps don't have the experience to understand what the customer really needs and how to get the requirements, or perhaps they don't have the authority to make decisions about the priority of the requirements. A Product Owner has to be creative and maybe a little bit innovative, and think about how best to represent the actual users of the product or service.

A product's success hinges on the quality of information to the team. A product 'champion' who has empathy for the customers must provide leadership to the team, as in Scrum's Product Owner role. My own research into success factors for organizations wanting to become agile (Re Turner 2018) found that having an empowered Product Owner who communicated the vision and focus of the product to the team was a critical success factor. Sadly, my experience of working with organizations that are struggling to become agile is that they don't have a committed, empowered person in that role, regardless of whether or not the title Product Owner is adopted.

Nevertheless, having a strong Product Owner does not mean that the team is now directed at task level to remove all thinking from their work. The team should be involved in the whole development cycle and make recommendations to the Product Owner. I describe this to my clients as a conversation and not one-way communication. Often when we refer to 'the team', we're talking about the development team. I prefer Scrum's broader definition of Scrum Team, which includes the Product Owner, Development Team, and Scrum Master. This is the unit that's needed, at a minimum, to deliver great products on time and with high quality.

A large-scale literature review of the research on the use of Agile frameworks showed that, in 2009, the highest-rated success factors were customer satisfaction and customer commitment to the team's success (Misra et al. 2009). Further research into the success factors for using Agile frameworks shows that interaction with customers, and relationships with external partners, both of which are to provide input into product development, lead to successful outcomes (Bermejo et al. 2014). Alahyari and colleagues (2017) reported time to market as the most important benefit realized by organizations through using Agile frameworks. Product development, broadly speaking, has the same success measures. Successful product development teams 'accelerate the product development lifecycle' with quicker time-to-market and high customer satisfaction (Edmondson and Nembhard 2009).

The Agile literature defines a product development team as one that includes a Product Owner, as in a Product Owner in the Scrum Team (Schwaber and Sutherland 2017) with daily, face-to-face contact (Beck et al. 2001). The large-scale literature review cited above (Misra et al. 2009) reveals how the Scrum Product Owner role is important to success, together with investing time with the Product Owner into learning how to refine requirements to a point where product development teams can build a meaningful increment of product (Dikert et al. 2016). Mature Agile teams allow requirements to change, care about delivering quality products to customers, and deliver against perceived outcomes expected from customers (Fontana et al. 2014). Successful teams have 'clear purpose, strategy, process, and vision' and 'engage with all their critical stakeholders' (Hawkins 2017). Research on Agile teams showed that when teams didn't have commitment from business stakeholders to provide input into the requirements of management and planning, organizations realized less value from agile methods (Dikert et al. 2016).

The Scrum Guide references self-organizing teams that have commitment and focus to product development goals and have support from management to get the job done in whichever way the team decides (Schwaber and Sutherland 2017). In the world of software development, this was a departure from the heavyweight processes that had been used to plan, develop, and quality-check new products. From the 1990s, the emphasis was on how we recognized that human factors are important for creating valuable products (Rigby et al. 2016). But new-product development teams that are successful in complex, uncertain, and ambiguous environments must be more than simply groups of people working towards a common purpose (Grobman 2005). With a challenging objective, a tight timeframe, trust and empowerment from management, knowledge workers can innovate beyond the ability of teams that follow prescriptive processes (Takeuchi and Nonaka 1986). Agile development methods recognize the growing awareness that teams operating in complex environments need to learn continuously about the products they develop and adapt the team's processes and communication if they are to be effective.

In today's organizations, the design, development, and production of new products is a fast-paced interdisciplinary endeavour – calling for teams rather than highly structured functional organizations to get the job done (Edmondson and Nembhard 2009).

Effective teams share purpose and vision (Senge 2006; Hawkins 2017), but for teams to engage in knowledge work required to deliver innovative products, they need the ability to do more than just complete tasks towards a common purpose. They need to self-organize, to be able to create products of high value (Takeuchi and Nonaka 1986; Katzenbach and Smith 1993; Stacey 1995). Edmondson (2019) says, 'Most leaders would be well served by stopping to reflect on the purpose that motivates them and makes the organization's work meaningful to the broader community. Having done so, they should ask themselves how often and how vigorously they are conveying this compelling rationale for the work to others'. When purpose is a clear motivator for teams, leaders can't afford not to be clear themselves on this purpose, because they need to communicate it effectively and in a timely manner to their teams.

## Create a product vision statement

We know that having a sense of purpose – as individuals or in teams and groups – is highly motivational. For agile organizations, one of the main aims is to be customer focused. Any one of the many tools used for identifying and refining the team's purpose will be useful here.

Having a clear picture of the initiative's product vision helps the team and Product Owner stay focused on delivery of value, instead of the delivery of tasks. It's a crucial part of outcome-based planning, as discussed earlier in the book. It gives the team purpose and is an important success factor for teams. Outcome-based planning uses business outcome statements for each expected release to stay on track, instead of a task list or to-do list disguised as a Product Backlog. Agile projects plan from the 'top down', meaning they start with the product vision and a high-level idea, evolving into a list of high-level requirements that define the project scope but do not have enough detail to build the product.

One of the best tools I know for creating customer focus and helping to focus the team at the same time is Roman Pichler's Product Vision Board. This facilitation tool helps a cross-functional team create a product vision statement by collectively brainstorming the target group, needs, product, and business goals of the proposed project. You can find out more about how to use the tool from Roman's website (see the reference list for a URL to his website). While this is certainly not a behavioural change tool from a professional coach's toolkit, it is a popular and effective tool used in Agile teams to create purpose, one of the critical success factors for teams generally, and a prerequisite for team focus.

# Cross-silo leadership

I wish I didn't have to write this section of the book. I wish we no longer had silos in our organizations – they are fundamentally working against us in the same way that petrol and diesel cars are working against our health and the environment. And, like the killer cars that we assume we need and can't live without, we assume we need highly structured and siloed organizations. Despite growing evidence to the contrary, some organizations can't seem to let go of traditional organizational structures. Challenging such a fundamental idea about or organization charts questions our basic assumptions about 'how we get things done here'. The root cause of our ignorance of corporate organizational structures can be thought of as cultural (Schein 2009), where people want to sit with and be part of a sub-culture of their function: for example, finance, marketing, or HR. These different sub-cultures, Schein says, originate from the different background and training of people in each of those professions. These organizational structures have not caught up to the demands of today's knowledge work, which demands that options and solutions are generated with a diverse team that has capacity to learn-while-doing (Edmondson 2012).

Casciaro et al. (2019) describe 'horizontal leadership' as being more important than 'vertical leadership' for enabling the learning and adapting that's important for today's companies in competitive markets. The researchers asked people in all kinds of organizations whether they prioritize vertical or horizontal relationships — the answer was almost always 'vertical'. But when they asked people, 'Which relationships are most important for creating value for customers?', the answer was 'horizontal'. Building those relationships, they say, involves learning about people in other business units, and relating to them. To build such relationships, teams need to:

- **Develop and deploy cultural brokers.** Teams that learn fastest are able to work cross-culturally, and often there is at least one person in a team who is able to cross cultural lines to create a bridge. I have observed this working very well – unconsciously – at a client's where I was an Agile Coach. The business analyst for a team regularly summarized what he heard from an offshore team for the benefit of the onshore people sitting in the room with him. This attempt at bridging had many benefits, including opening the door for clarifying meaning by both groups separated by the teleconference system. In addition to benefitting people in the room to hear what was said a second time, it was the attempt to check understanding by courageously attempting to summarize what he understood that gave additional benefit to creating this bridge.

- **Encourage people to ask the right questions.** As a coach, your skills with using open questions, curiosity, probing questions, and looking for exceptions in a narrative will help you ask compelling questions that enable other people's thinking.

- **Get people to see the world through others' eyes.** Leaders should encourage staff to understand others' point of view. I propose using the Meta Mirror technique with coaches, which sets up a simulation in which you ask your coachee to step into the position of another in order to see the world from their point of view. The Meta Mirror technique has its origins in Gestalt and was later adopted in NLP, whose first practitioners observed Gestalt therapists.

- **Broaden your employees' vision.** Leaders should encourage staff to meet and work with people at all levels of other functional groups and business units in order to gain a bigger picture of the people and work they're engaged with.

### Achieving emotional commitment

Working with diverse stakeholders across organizational boundaries often involves selling an idea, and an effective way to do this is to appeal to people's heads as well as hearts. To create emotional commitment, ensure that your coachee can explain the idea or plan in its context, explain why the approach is important for the organization and the individuals involved, create commitment to the idea by finding ways of creating early wins, and ensure that they can instil belief in individuals for affecting the plan by involving them early and often.

### Meta Mirror

Coaches can work with coachees to develop empathy for other people by asking them to step into another's shoes. A technique that I've used many times in my coaching work is Meta Mirror, described below. There are different approaches to this; I have described here my preferred version, though you will find different versions of this and you should adapt it as you see fit.

Place two chairs opposite each other and invite your coachee to sit in one of them – this is the 'first position'. Say to your coachee, 'Imagine that your colleague is sitting in front of you now, in that chair, and say whatever you want to him'. When your coachee has finished speaking, ask them to stand, and ask if they're ready to continue. If they say 'yes', ask your coachee to sit in the other chair. Ask them to adopt the colleague's physical body language by asking the coachee to imagine how the other person sits, their gestures, and facial expressions. Then ask your coachee to put themselves into their colleague's shoes, the 'second position', and respond to the information that was given by the person in the 'first position'. Observe any changes in your coachee in their experience of the second position. Ask your coachee to step away from the two chairs and look back at them, the 'third position', and ask them to notice what's taking place between the two people. Use appropriate open questions to stimulate your coachee's thinking. Finally, ask your coachee to sit in the first position and invite them to say something to their colleague.

## Inspiring trust

In an increasingly uncertain and fragile world, it may be tempting for your coachee to seek power to give a feeling of control. By contrast, they describe trust as being longer-lasting and more flexible than power-seeking behaviour. Leaders should practise these ten behaviours to gain the trust leading to agility that leaders desire. Interestingly, three of these are also Scrum values – noted within this list:

1 Fairness
2 Dependability
3 Respect (also in Scrum)
4 Openness (also in Scrum)
5 Courage (also in Scrum)
6 Unselfishness
7 Competence
8 Supportiveness
9 Empathy
10 Compassion

## Connector managers

Connector managers lead with the whole organization in mind, helping teams see their work through the eyes of customers, business partners, or suppliers.

Managers who connect employees to each other build better talent. That's what Gartner analyst Sari Wilde said in a podcast, where she asserted that connector managers build better talent (HBR Ideacast 2019b), which correlates to behaviours needed in organizations that want to become agile.

She described different types of managers:

- Teachers – 'develop employees based on their own skills and experience'.
- Cheerleaders – 'take a hands-off approach to development' and 'encourage self-development'. They delegate support to other people for coaching, mentoring, and input.
- Always-on – 'they have good intentions and want to provide ongoing coaching and feedback'. She said many companies are promoting this approach.
- Connectors – give 'targeted and specific feedback' when they have the expertise; 'connect employees with others who are better suited to provide coaching and development'; and 'are known for creating a trusting and transparent environment that encourages peer to peer feedback'. They facilitate the employees' development while encouraging input from others. They

are still involved, unlike a Cheerleader. They prepare the employee for the conversation – help set clear goals – and follow up with a conversation to facilitate reflection. Sari Wilde calls this 'warm up and cool down' conversations, aka book-ends.

Connector managers: (1) ask questions about people's interests to understand them at a deep level, creating a 'one-to-one connection', asking the right kinds of questions to understand their 'motivations, interests, and goals'; (2) create an 'open and transparent environment' so that team members can develop each other, taking advantage of each other's skills; and (3) develop the organization connection – managers have the self-awareness to realize that as individuals, they don't have all the skills that their employees need. They help their employees make connections around the organization to get skills and help when needed. They teach their employees to be good networkers. This is about teaching employees to be resourceful, not about the manager having their own large network. When teams have connector managers, they 'tend to be more trusting and open with each other'. So feedback is coming from multiple people, not just one person – the manager.

An article on the website of the World Economic Forum written by the global chief executive officer of Deloitte, Punit Renjen (2019), says that the so-called Fourth Industrial Revolution requires four types of leaders: Social Supers, Data-Driven Decisives, Disruption Drivers, and Talent Champions. These are leaders who will 'thrive' and be able to create business strategies and utilize technology to achieve business results.

# Working with the systems around the team

Systems thinking requires us to see wholes. The approach is the complete opposite to problem-solving techniques that require us to break down an issue into its component parts in order to understand the issue and address the components. When we are addressing organizational impediments, the system of interest is often a business unit in the organization, or a team, or a network of teams.

Think of some of the systemic issues in society and consider the complexity involved in trying to provide solutions to them. Crime, income inequality, environmental degradation, and healthcare for all are just a few of the complex issues that politicians and other leaders have tried to fix but without a sustainable solution. Due to the very nature of the issues, it is very difficult to identify the root causes and even more difficult to identify, prioritize, and implement solutions.

Organizations are systems, and the issues that help or hinder them to move quickly and gain competitive advantage are sometimes difficult to see and even harder to change. Add to this the influence of organizational culture and it is easy to see why so many organizations find it difficult to do in practice what individuals in the same organizations know needs to get done – to adapt to a changing business environment.

## Make issues visible on the Kanban board

Look for examples of the seven Lean Wastes in your Kanban board and you'll find the starting point for identifying organizational impediments. To me, this tool is a way to get feedback about the working environment – specifically the bottlenecks that slow down product development efforts. I am disappointed when I see teams grossly under-utilize the board as nothing more than a task board of work that has been assigned by someone and is never to be looked at by the team. When used as a true pull system, your Kanban board reveals bottlenecks that can be traced to issues in the systems of which your team is a member.

## Constellations

Coach Hazel Chapman, who uses Constellations with her clients, spoke to me about how she uses the approach for helping groups understand their relationships to stakeholders. Constellations was created by John Whittington (2016) based on the work of Bert Hellinger, for understanding systemic relationships. Chapman describes the activity to her groups as a 'stakeholder map' which can include anyone inside or outside the organization. She says many business people find the activity strange at first because they are thinkers whereas Constellations is a somatic activity.

As with much of coaching, the group picks an issue to work on together. The facilitated activity is fundamentally somatic – it uses physical relationships and movement to understand existing human relationships. The technique can reveal what needs to change, coming from physical movement in a space (a conference room, for example) relative to others, all of whom have taken the role of an actor in the system. Chapman says, 'When it comes to stakeholders, it's almost the only thing I've found that works'.

It's a little more directive than coaching – more about stating observations and asking people to move around the room than asking open questions. The facilitator keeps in mind the constellations principles to notice when the principles have been broken. She recommends coaches get training in facilitating using Constellations.

## Awareness of the system

Here's an exercise I designed and use with groups on awareness of the system. I ask group members to write a short case study of their organization, using the following questions. The questions were intended to be used as a starting point for understanding the extent to which participants think systemically about their organization. An article in *Forbes* magazine (Chavez 2019) inspired many of the questions:

**Capability:** What can we uniquely do or offer that other companies cannot?

**Caring:** What motivates and energizes our people? What drives their empathy for customers and stakeholders?

**Context:** What is happening in the world that allows us to make a contribution? In other words, why might the world need our capabilities?

**Customers:** What do the people we serve want and need, not just in terms of products and services, but also experiences?

**Calling:** Putting everything else together, what are we ultimately called to do? This is really the big question and a culmination of the exploration through the other lenses.

### Current issues

- If you stand back from your business, where are the places where projects stall?
- Where is communication blocked?
- Where do people or groups persistently fail to rise to their potential?
- How often do you or others blame the issue on personalities or interpersonal conflicts?

## McKinsey 7S

The McKinsey 7S framework provides a lens through which to evaluate the balance of aspects of Agile transformation. The intention of using this framework is to show that focusing on the so-called 'hard' aspects of organizational change, particularly structure, isn't enough to make your change efforts stick. The McKinsey consultants created the framework in reaction to what they observed as reliance on changes to organizational structure to implement business strategy. Beliefs of the time held that when the organization's strategy was sound, all that was needed was to implement it with the right structure. However, 'the main problem in strategy [was] getting it done', according to the framework's authors Robert Waterman, Jr., Thomas Peters, and Julien Phillips. This led to a holistic view of organizational change that included the so-called 'soft' aspects of change in the framework: Style, Staff, Skills, and the overarching Shared Values.

## McKinsey 7S activity

With a whiteboard and the seven aspects of the McKinsey 7S framework, I asked one participant to read their case study and the remaining group members to annotate the giant-sized model with what they heard, so that they can build a kind of visual model of the reader's attention to aspects of their organization.

This approach was based on my MSc research in 2017/18, whereby I coded transcribed interviews and recorded instances of key words and themes to aspects of 7S for each participant. The result was that I got an impression of where each research participant put their attention, with the assumption that the individual was representative of the group and culture in which they work.

**Figure 8.1** Mental map of the system using 7S

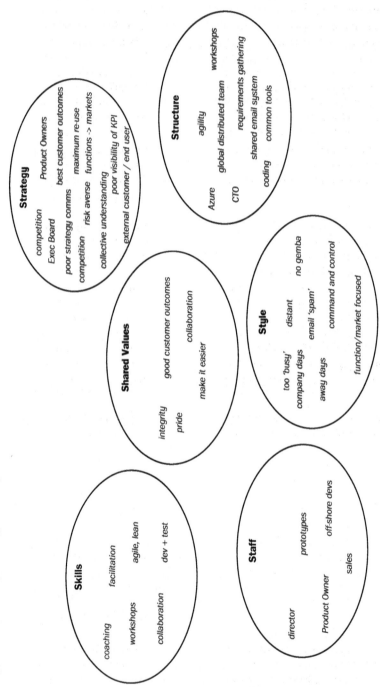

## Approaches for better stakeholder relationships

Recommendations for areas that typically receive less attention but which are nonetheless important for a balanced relationship with stakeholders in the system around the team in the organization include:

### Increase attention to strategy

- Coach Agile teams and leaders to develop a shared mental map that expresses the business vision effectively for self-organized decision-making within Agile teams.
- Facilitate workshops to identify the organization's goals, vision, and purpose, and translate those into goals, vision, and purpose for the Agile teams.
- Make workshop outputs transparent by generating artefacts from the workshops that are highly visible (Schwaber and Sutherland 2017); for example, posted on walls in common areas.
- Commit to ways of receiving feedback, and prioritize items to focus on now.
- Identify beliefs and past experiences that prevent positive relationships among stakeholders and Agile team members, using a Constellations approach.
- If Agile team members do not see the big picture, use visualization techniques so the team can get an overall picture of the goal.

*Suggested coaching questions*:

- ○ Leaders: What beliefs and attitudes do we have that help or hinder our relationships with members of product development teams?
- ○ Teams: What beliefs and attitudes do we have that help or hinder our relationships with business and Product Owners?
- ○ Leaders: How can we increase the importance of Product Owners to commit to working with Agile teams, so as to communicate our business vision?

### Increase attention to working style

- Coach leaders to adopt behaviours that encourage experimentation.
- Allow teams to self-organize, within boundaries, to create valuable products through customer feedback and continuous improvement.
- Coach Agile team members to identify helpful interactions that allow them to work creatively.
- Engage the leaders involved in influencing product development teams to identify blocks to releasing control of detailed planning and execution to the teams doing the work. Examine 'patterns of interaction' and 'quality of engagement', using a Gestalt approach, and 'how the team is making contact, or not, with important stakeholders in the wider organization' (Leary-Joyce 2014).

*Suggested coaching questions:*

- o In which areas of product development do the individuals have more experience (than you) with development of this product or service?
- o Think of a project or initiative in which team members seemed to 'go the extra mile' to make the project/initiative a success. What were the conditions that contributed the most to the high motivation of team members to be successful?
- o How would a greater belief in self-organization change your actions as a manager, coach, or organizational development practitioner?

### Increase attention to shared values

- Facilitate workshops to identify the shared values held by the teams in the organization. How are these similar or different to the values espoused by the Agile Manifesto?
- Coach the teams and organization to identify behaviours that help and/or hinder their ability to meet product development goals.

*Suggested coaching questions:*

- o In what ways do our values support our vision for the products we develop here?
- o In what ways do we demonstrate the organization's values, as a team?
- o In what ways do I demonstrate the organization's values, as a team member?
- o In what ways do I demonstrate the organization's values, as a leader?

---

### Reflective questions for Lens 5

1 In which aspects of the McKinsey 7S framework have you been working as a coach? Which areas require more of your attention in order to support your coachees in a balanced approach to change?
2 Record a meeting of a team that you coach or work with – seeking their permission first. Play back the recording and record instances of discussion about each of the aspects of 7S. In which of the aspects does the team spend the most time?
3 If your client built in ways of sense-checking planned new features with their customers, what could they learn to shorten learning cycles between product releases?
4 What are the benefits of gaining team members' emotional commitment to an initiative?

# Lens 6 – Wider systemic context

**Why you should read this chapter**

- A major benefit of using Agile frameworks is derived from the organization's ability to adapt quickly to changing external conditions.
- To anticipate and respond to changes in the wider systemic context, leaders and teams must learn to widen their awareness of global trends that have local implications.

*Lens Six – Wider systemic context (PESTLE)*

*The client organization, which I will not identify, operates in a highly competitive market that is subject to price fluctuations caused by the availability of refined natural resources, seasonal consumer demand, regulation and intense competition, some from low-cost entrants during the last ten years. Operating in a highly volatile, competitive, and uncertain market likely put senior management under tremendous pressure to deliver projects on time.*

I've seen examples at nearly all of the clients I've worked with who feel pressure at the top (due to external forces), which is then passed down from C-level executives to the top team, to managers, to their teams. There's a lot at stake from misjudging consumer trends, creating exposure to risk from supply chain uncertainty and price fluctuations, or unforeseen competition. Considering the pace of change brought about by new technology, it's no longer acceptable for organizations to adopt a wait-and-see approach to new product and service offerings.

## The vision and focus of Agile organizations

We know that successful organizations have vision and focus. So what do Agile organizations focus on specifically?

Research by Dave Ullrich, professor at the University of Michigan Ross School of Business (HBR Ideacast 2019c), describes organizations that move fast and scale as 'market-oriented ecosystems'. The old mental model of an organization is of a hierarchy. They were built for clarity-of-role – and they were 'great in a world of stability'. Hierarchical organizations don't respond to change. The newer companies in the researchers' work can innovate and move rapidly. They have a few things in common. They are market-oriented, and have 'cells' like a holding company. Successful companies have an 'ecosystem' that requires the relationships among the cells connects each of the cells.

Successful companies, which can adapt to change, have these capabilities:

- A vision with a platform in the middle, with cells around the middle
- External sensing – what is happening in the world?
- Customer anticipation – what are customers buying?
- Innovation – how do we innovate our products and business model?
- Agility – 'how do we move quickly to make that happen' and 'focus on the future' is how the researchers defined 'agility'.

It comes down to information sharing across 'cells', which could also be considered business units that speak to the rest of the organization – across business units. Older companies, which might have risen to the top with economies of scale in their supply chain, didn't have these new capabilities. What gets in the way is our outdated mental models about what an organization should look like. First and foremost, work with leaders to empower others to create human relationships across cells, instead of maintaining control.

## Creativity and experimentation

I wish there was a one-size-fits-all coaching approach for developing innovation but there isn't. The Agile world is full of paradoxes ('Simplicity – the art of maximizing the work not done – is essential'; Beck et al. 2001), and so is the business of human relationships. Remember the common advice that to have more influence, speak less and listen more. To me, no part of this book is more paradoxical than developing innovation. To make the truly great breakthroughs, we need to learn from experience and listen to the customer continuously. There are no huge breakthrough moments, just trial and error. Elvin Turner suggests in *Be Less Zombie* (2020) that to encourage innovation and creativity, take the pressure off by relying on a process to help you do the work. Anxiety is a killer of creativity. On a behavioural level, we want to give courage to people to link disparate concepts and voice their wild and crazy ideas. I love the spirit of Liberating Structures in enabling people at all levels to have that voice. I've already mentioned in the Introduction that one of the most prominent management thinkers, Peter Drucker, said that knowledge workers are the ones who have the most potential to impact how a business understands how to delight customers.

*What is experimentation?*

Experimentation – or learning to accept that failure is a learning opportunity – is the new normal, as illustrated in the HBR Live Event 'Leading Transformation to the Intelligent Enterprise' (HBR Webcast 2019)

People in the Agile world use the phrase 'fail fast' and I think this is the same as experimentation. A 'fail fast' mindset means that failures are learning opportunities. I also sometimes refer to this as 'learning by doing', which acknowledges that talking about a problem can get the team to a point but doesn't prove anything.

Jeanne Ross, Principal Research Scientist at the Center for Information Systems Research at MIT Sloan School of Management, says that many organizations talk about failure as an ingredient to eventual success. A better way of thinking about learning from experience she said, is 'The most successful organizations aren't the ones who fail, they're the ones who experiment'. Experimentation, she said, not failure, is how we learn what works.

## Generate creative options and solutions

Agile frameworks, especially Scrum, refer to empiricism or making decisions based on experience. Bossons et al. (2012) call this 'heuristics', or using experience where a structured approach won't work due to the novelty of the situation. In this instance, which is where many companies in fast-moving markets find themselves, they say stick to the organization's desired outcomes and learn from experience to find out what they're doing that helps or hinders them. The resemblance to Scrum's inspect-and-adapt cycles were mentioned in the iterative development chapter in this book. Bosson et al. also remind us of well-known but sometimes forgotten approaches that have been with us for many years: mind mapping, vertical and lateral thinking, questioning, and brainstorming.

Finally, Bossons et al. (2012) summarize an eight-step approach for 'deep dive prototyping' that has an uncanny resemblance to GV's Design Sprints created by Jake Knapp and John Zeratsky. The steps are:

1  Build a diverse and varied team
2  Define the challenge
3  Visit experts
4  Share ideas
5  Brainstorm and vote
6  Develop a fast prototype
7  Test and refine the prototype
8  Focus on the prototype and produce a solution

## GV Sprint

Similarly, the GV Sprint 5-day approach follows a process of listening to users, voting, and prototyping to generate a viable idea quickly. Its five process steps are Map, Sketch, Decide, Prototype, and Test, one for each day of a five-day business week.

## Lean Startup

I deliberately left out Lean Startup from the Agile frameworks chapter. To me, Lean Startup is all mindset and very little method. In fact, the essence of Lean Startup – to build the smallest complete version of a product and 'test' it by releasing it to market and then learning from experience – is present in all of the methods in Chapter 2. Eric Ries did a terrific job of both distilling the essence and value of iterative development and making it widely accessible to companies in any sector that builds products or services.

The Lean Startup learning cycle is the same in concept as the feedback loops presented earlier, with an emphasis on learning from an actual product released to your target customers. MVP means minimum viable product in Lean Startup and it is at the heart of what gets released to the market. More often than not, I hear groups use minimum viable product to mean all of the must-have features that they believe, with a waterfall mindset, that need to be built before anything can be released or shipped. When MVP is used incorrectly it indicates that people's mindsets have not shifted. It is an improper use of the term, shoehorned into the old mindsets.

## Creative thinking

Elspeth McFadzean (1999) analyzed techniques for creative thinking and categorized these into paradigm stretching and paradigm breaking techniques. Paradigm stretching refers to thinking more expansively on a topic; paradigm breaking is imagining new and unseen options or solutions to problems. These go far beyond well-known brainstorming techniques that draw on current patterns of thinking (paradigm preserving). Paradigm-stretching techniques are the most challenging for a team to participate in, so attention must be given to the psychological safety of the group members. Paradigm-preserving techniques such as force field analysis and Disney Creative Strategy, presented earlier in the book, are effective in many situations but nevertheless ask people to describe what they know to be true. Paradigm-stretching and -breaking approaches ask participants to 'think outside the box'.

### *Paradigm stretching – metaphors*

Group members can use metaphors, another paradigm-stretching technique, to create a fantasy situation so that they can gain a new perspective on the problem. This technique can be used in the following way:

1  Develop a problem statement and write it on a flipchart.
2  Ask the group to select a metaphor category or stipulate a category: for example, the journey metaphor.

3 Invite each individual to describe the situation using the metaphor category. Stipulate whether the description should cover the present situation or the ideal situation.
4 Ask participants to use the descriptions developed by each team member to generate new ideas.
5 Ask the group to relate these ideas back to the problem statement.

A number of different types of metaphors can be useful for solving problems and finding opportunities. These include nature metaphors, vehicle metaphors, creational metaphors, and journey metaphors. Again, this method requires some imagination on the part of the group. Developing metaphors may be difficult for some people and requires practice. Nevertheless, once they master it, they can produce very creative results.

As the facilitator, create a set of cards, each with a metaphor chosen to create expansive thinking. Some examples are: world travel, jazz music, the Olympics. These are best offered on cards that a team member can select from, without preference. You can also of course ask participants to come up with their own metaphors and write them on blank index cards and then select blind from those. A virtual version is possible by using an online whiteboard (the one in Zoom works just as well as the slicker ones in tools such as Miro) to capture people's metaphors as they shout them out. The community created content in Miroverse has boards you can use for this. Then ask participants to use the 'stamp' in Annotations to vote on the ones they want to use for the activity. (Basic facilitation tip: calibrate the number of votes for each person to the number of items and participants, so that a clear 'winner' will emerge from voting.)

Now the team members can do the real work – to stretch their idea of the problem using the metaphor they selected. An adaptation of McFadzean's metaphors technique (1999) is for members of the group to pair up to discuss the issue in the lens of the metaphor the group chose. Each pair uses the same metaphor. Use a plenary discussion for each pair to present their new view of the issue through the metaphor lens.

*Paradigm breaking – rich pictures*

Rich pictures is another technique that can help participants look at problems from a totally different perspective. It can change the patterns of thinking within the group. Rich pictures can be used as follows:

1 Develop a problem statement and write it on a flipchart.
2 Ask each individual to draw two pictures. The pictures may be metaphors for the situation: for example, vehicles or animals. The first drawing should be a picture of how the participant would like to see the situation in the future. The second picture should be a drawing of how the participant sees the present situation.

3 Ask each participant to first describe the picture of the present situation. Not only should he or she describe the picture, but also the properties of the objects drawn and why they were drawn that way. Next, the individual should describe the picture of the future, again including the properties and the relationships of the objects.

4 Ask the participants to generate new ideas based on the descriptions.

Rich pictures is a useful technique because the group can very quickly see what each member's perception of the problem is and what he or she would like in the future. Moreover, a picture can very effectively show a vast amount of information, such as patterns, relationships, and properties. It can easily be shared with the other group members, and they can all see the problem in its entirety in a single glance. This method can also be used as a quick icebreaker at the beginning of a session. The group, however, needs to be persuaded of the technique's effectiveness before participating, because many people feel inhibited and embarrassed about their poor drawing skills. The facilitator needs to convince the group that pictures do not have to be works of art as long as they make sense to their creators and can be described to the group. The facilitator needs to be skilled at teasing information out of the participants as they describe their pictures. There are times when participants leave out information because the facilitator has failed to ask the correct questions.

Commonly used by systems practitioners, and developed by Peter Checkland in his Soft Systems Methodology (The Open University 2020), rich pictures help a team gain understanding of a complex issue which would be difficult to put into words or to understand completely. When I ask workshop participants to draw pictures, some people are resistant, saying, 'but I can't draw!'. Acknowledge their objections and proceed confidently with the activity. The less you as facilitator make of the work to be done, the easier it will be for them. As each participant describes the current situation and their desired future state, ask questions so that the group can gain clarification and indeed so that the person can gain more understanding of what they think.

## Develop listening skills

There is an opportunity for coaches to sit in on some meetings such as product visioning, retrospectives, or planning meetings and, by invitation from the team, to support team members by helping them to improve their questioning and listening skills. Similar to how we work with coachees one to one, we can model effective questioning for the team to ask to hear more about what has been said, as well as listening for what is not being said. Similarly, Jake Knapp says that the GV Sprint method he and John Zeratsky created at Google includes broad questioning by team members to help the idea's originator think more expansively (IDEO Futures 2016). Support your teams to think of questioning as a way to become more expansive and help develop ideas, as opposed to using questions to negatively challenge or slip in personal views. The purpose is to ensure on the most fundamental level that people are heard.

# External sensing

External sensing is about taking in information from disparate industry sectors, disciplines, sources, and domains to spot trends. It's true the amount of information available to us is greater than ever, and with it the possibility to see trends emerging. (To get a feel for the range of sources mined for this book, see the Bibliography.) Sense-making requires leaders to encourage dialogue in groups to take advantage of groups' natural sense-making ability and, as mentioned elsewhere in this book, to get teams to do more the work of making sense of trends. Part of sense-making is the courage to try new approaches and experiment with new ideas.

Richard Pascale says external sensing is the ability to draw on diverse sources of information to create a picture of trends, and to apply the picture to your business context for making strategic decisions. In the uncertain and changing environments in which we work, external sensing is important but doesn't let us predict the future. It helps us avoid the trap of continuing to do the thing that made us successful even while the indicators we need to change are all around us (Pascale 1990).

Below, I present three coaching approaches to help your clients focus on the future and expected outcomes. Agility, said Dave Ullrich in an HBR Ideacast (2019c), is about 'focus on the future'. Nevertheless, I've already shown through- out this book that 'Agile' development requires a mindset in addition to pro- cesses that allow us to adapt when unexpected change occurs. My cautionary word for using the three approaches here is this: planning for the future requires conscious attention on what has changed since the plan was made. And some- thing will change. Unless you choose to use Agile frameworks as a vanity exer- cise, you're using one of the Agile development frameworks because you work in a business that is subject to change and uncertainty.

## Responding to change

David Snowden's Cynefin framework remains one of the most enduring although somewhat abstract ways we have to understand the so-called 'planning para- dox', as Mary Poppendieck calls it. The paradox is that despite our best inten- tions, plans are aspirational and don't reflect reality for long after it's created.

Snowden's model tells us that in complex environments it is not possible to pre- dict the future. The best way to get a new product designed, built, and delivered to market comes from 'emergent practice', meaning we learn as we go. 'Best practice', meaning there is one ideal way to get things done that is guaranteed to work – which doesn't exist in complex environments. Sorry to burst your bubble on that one! I remember reading a blog post a few years ago by Mike Cohn who described what we do, when practising Agile development well, as 'good practice'. I like to call it 'good enough'.

The organization will experience more commitment to the scenarios, a vision for the future, and well-formed outcomes – the focus of the next approach – when you work with a group instead of individuals. Your facilitation skills will be called upon here.

## Scenario thinking

Writing scenarios helps to make apparent the possible causes of change. The benefit of doing this is to explore several possible futures, and to understand risks more clearly than if we only planned for what is known. In *Coaching Essentials* (2012), Bossons et al. recommend involving a diverse group of people from all levels of the organization to get the greatest amount of input. You may want to use one of the creative facilitation techniques as part of your idea generation in the Scenario Thinking process. The facilitation process they recommend is:

- *Exploring the scenarios.* Discuss the forces of change in your business context. They could be internal forces or external forces. PESTLE is a good model for identifying external forces – see the example in Part 1 of this book.
- *Developing the scenarios.* Narrow the list of forces by selecting three of the forces from the previous step that relate to a specific time period. Describe the possible outcomes from each. How are they related? This will help you build one scenario for each outcome you identified.
- *Analyzing the scenarios.* The purpose of this step is to further examine the forces that could lead to different future outcomes. As facilitator, create questions that help your participants examine the strength of each force, listing more if necessary.
- *Using the scenarios.* This final step asks participants to work backwards from each outcome to brainstorm mitigating steps that the group should take to recognize the scenario when it occurs, and the mitigation steps.

Jeremy Bentham, Head of Scenarios from Shell, is a risk management expert. Interviewed by Evan Davis on 'Planning for uncertainty' on BBC Radio 4, he described how his team at Shell plans for unpredictable outcomes, using scenarios (BBC 2019).

## Visualization and future orientation

We saw earlier that Agile-style project planning is based on desired future outcomes and not tasks. This approach can help a group create a business vision that guides the efforts of product development initiatives and programmes of work.

- Decide what you want.
- Trust your intuition. As described earlier in this book, intuition can be a shortcut to complex knowledge you already have.
- Test your assumptions and tap into the future.
- Get people to understand and support the vision.
- Remember the characteristics of progressive views of the future: powerful, communicable, desirable and realistic, focused, and adaptive. Challenge the flexibility of your approach by asking the group for ways that the vision can fail.

(Bossons et al. 2012)

**Reflective questions for Lens 6**

1  Use the PESTLE model to brainstorm the external sources of change and uncertainty for your client's organization. What would others in the organization add to it?
2  Where does creativity come from?
3  How can you model good listening skills for your clients and draw attention to the benefits of listening to create empathy and promote generative discourse?

# Bibliography

Adkins, L. (2010) *Coaching Agile Teams*, Kindle edition. Upper Saddle River, NJ: Addison-Wesley.

Agile Business Consortium (2017) *Agile Project Management Handbook v2.0*. High Wycombe: Agile Business Consortium.

Agile Coaching Institute (2017) *Agile Coaching Competency Framework*. Available at: https://www.agilecoachinginstitute.com/agile-coaching-resources/.

Alahyari, H., Svensson, R.B. and Gorschek, T. (2017) A study of value in agile software development organizations, *Journal of Systems and Software*, 125: 271–288.

Anderson, D.J. (2010) *Kanban: Successful Evolutionary Change for Your Technology Business*, Kindle edition. Sequim, WA: Blue Hole Press.

Andres, H.P. (2013) Team cognition using collaborative technology: A behavioural analysis, *Journal of Managerial Psychology*, 28 (1): 38–54.

Argyris, C. (2002) Teaching smart people how to learn, *Harvard Business Review*, May/June. Available at: https://hbr.org/1991/05/teaching-smart-people-how-to-learn (accessed 11 February 2021).

BBC (2019) Planning for uncertainty, *The Bottom Line*, BBC Radio 4. Available at: https://www.bbc.co.uk/programmes/m0003jsm (accessed 5 March 2020).

BBC (2020) How we work now – lessons from lockdown, *The Bottom Line*, BBC Radio 4. Available at: https://www.bbc.co.uk/programmes/m000knj2 (accessed 11 August 2020).

Beck, K. (2005) *Extreme Programming Explained*, 2nd edition, Kindle edition. Upper Saddle River, NJ: Pearson Education.

Beck, K., Beedle, M., van Bennekum, A., Cockburn, A., Cunningham, W., Fowler, M. et al. (2001) *The Manifesto for Agile Software Development*. Available at: http://agilemanifesto.org (accessed 10 October 2019).

Bens, I. (2018) *Facilitating with Ease! Core Skills for Facilitators, Team Leaders and Members, Managers, Consultants and Trainers*, 4th edition, Kindle edition. Hoboken, NJ: Wiley.

Bermejo, P.H. de S., Zambalde, A.L., Tonelli, A.O., Souza, S.A., Zuppo, L.A. and Rosa, P.L. (2014) Agile principles and achievement of success in software development: A quantitative study in Brazilian organizations, *Procedia Technology*, 16: 718–727.

Bierly, P.E., III, Stark, E.M. and Kessler, E.H. (2009) The moderating effects of virtuality on the antecedents and outcome of NPD Team Trust, *Journal of Product Innovation Management*, 26 (5): 551–565.

Boehm, B. (1984) Software engineering economics, *IEEE Transactions on Software Engineering*, 10 (1): 4–21.

Bossons, P., Kourdi, J. and Sartain, D. (2012) *Coaching Essentials: Practical, Proven Techniques for World-class Executive Coaching*, 2nd edition. London: Bloomsbury.

Bowman, S. (2009) *Training from the Back of the Room*. San Francisco, CA: Pfeiffer.

Brown, T. (2020) Why leadership is not about having all the answers, *IDEO*, podcast. Available at: https://www.ideou.com/blogs/inspiration/why-leadership-is-not-about-having-all-the-answers.

Cable, D. (2018) How humble leadership really works, *Harvard Business Review*, 23 April. Available at: https://hbr.org/2018/04/how-humble-leadership-really-works (accessed 21 April 2020).

Cameron, E. and Green, M. (2015) *Making Sense of Change Management: A Complete Guide to the Models, Tools and Techniques of Organizational Change*, Kindle edition. Philadelphia, PA: Kogan Page.

Casciaro, T., Edmondson, A. and Jang, S. (2019) Cross-silo leadership, *Harvard Business Review*, May/June. Available at: https://hbr.org/2019/05/cross-silo-leadership (accessed 28 April 2020).

Center for Servant Leadership (2020) What is Servant Leadership? South Orange, NJ: Center for Servant Leadership. Available at: https://www.greenleaf.org/what-is-servant-leadership/ (accessed 29 April 2020).

Cerminaro, D. (2019) A not-quite-textbook definition of systems design, *IDEO*, blog, 4 October. Available at: https://www.ideo.com/blog/a-not-quite-textbook-definition-of-systems-design (accessed 27 July 2020).

Chattopadhyay, S. (2020) Facilitating emergence and sensemaking in organizations, *Medium*, 26 July. Available at: https://medium.com/age-of-emergence/organization-design-71ab1b106c7a (accessed 11 February 2021).

Chavez, M. (2019) Need more agility? Focus on shared meaning, *Forbes*, 10 July. Available at: https://www.forbes.com/sites/michaelchavez/2019/07/10/need-more-agility-focus-on-shared-meaning/ (accessed 10 September 2019).

Christensen, C., Raynor, M. and McDonald, R. (2015) What is disruptive innovation?, *Harvard Business Review*, December. Available at: https://hbr.org/2015/12/what-is-disruptive-innovation (accessed 19 June 2020).

Church, Z. (2020) *TIAA CEO Roger Ferguson gets ideas from 'inside out' and 'outside in'*, Ideas Made to Matter, MIT Management Sloan School, 13 May. Available at: https://mitsloan.mit.edu/ideas-made-to-matter/tiaa-ceo-roger-ferguson-gets-ideas-from-inside-out-and-outside (accessed 8 July 2020).

Clutterbuck, D. (2002) How teams learn, *T+D: Talent Development*, 56 (3): 67–69.

Clutterbuck, D. (2007) *Coaching the Team at Work*, Kindle edition. London: Nicholas Brealey.

Davenport, T.H. and Spanyi, A. (2019) Digital transformation should start with customers, *MIT Sloan Management Review*, 8 October. Available at: https://sloanreview.mit.edu/article/digital-transformation-should-start-with-customers/ (accessed 27 July 2020).

Derby, E. and Larsen, D. (2006) *Agile Retrospectives: Making Good Teams Great*, Kindle edition. Dallas, TX: The Pragmatic Bookshelf.

Dikert, K., Paasivaara, M. and Lassenius, C. (2016) Challenges and success factors for large-scale agile transformations: A systematic literature review, *Journal of Systems and Software*, 119: 87–108.

Drucker, P. (1959) *The Landmarks of Tomorrow*. New York: Harper.

Drucker, P. (1999) Knowledge-worker productivity: The biggest challenge, *California Management Review*, 41 (2): 79–94.

Dubner, S.J. (2018) Here's why all your projects are always late – and what to do about it, *Freakonomics*, 7 March. Available at: https://freakonomics.com/podcast/project-management/ (accessed 11 February 2021).

Duffield, S. and Whitty, S.J. (2015) Developing a systemic lessons learned knowledge model for organisational learning through projects, *International Journal of Project Management*, 33 (2): 311–324.

Duhigg, C. (2016) What Google learned from its quest to build the perfect team, *The New York Times Magazine*, 25 February. Available at: https://www.nytimes.com/2016/02/28/magazine/what-google-learned-from-its-quest-to-build-the-perfect-team.html (accessed 13 June 2018).

Dweck, C. (2006) *Mindset: Changing the Way You Think to Fulfil Your Potential*, Kindle edition. London: Robinson.

Edmondson, A.C. (2012) *Teaming: How Organizations Learn, Innovate, and Compete in the Knowledge Economy*, Kindle edition. San Francisco, CA: Wiley.

Edmondson, A.C. (2019) *The Fearless Organization: Creating Psychological Safety in the Workplace for Learning, Innovation, and Growth*, Kindle edition. Hoboken, NJ: Wiley.

Edmondson, A.C. and Nembhard, I.M. (2009) Product development and learning in project teams: The challenges are the benefits, *Journal of Product Innovation Management*, 26 (2): 123–138.

Fontana, R.M., Fontana, I.M., da Rosa Garbuio, P.A., Reinehr, S. and Malucelli, A. (2014) Processes versus people: How should agile software development maturity be defined?, *Journal of Systems and Software*, 97: 140–155.

Fratto, N. (2019) Three ways to measure your adaptability – and how to improve it, *TED Talks*. Available at: https://www.ted.com/talks/natalie_fratto_3_ways_to_measure_your_adaptability_and_how_to_improve_it (accessed 15 March 2020).

Gibbs Howard, S. (2019) The three qualities leaders need in an uncertain future, *IDEO: The Journal*, 6 August. Available at: https://www.ideo.com/journal/the-three-qualities-leaders-need-in-an-uncertain-future (accessed 24 March 2020).

Gino, F. (2019) Cracking the code of sustained collaboration, *Harvard Business Review*, 1 November 2019. Available at: https://hbr.org/2019/11/cracking-the-code-of-sustained-collaboration (accessed 19 June 2020).

Gothelf, J. and Seiden, J. (2017) *Sense and Respond: How Successful Organizations Listen to Customers and Create New Products Continuously*, Kindle edition. Cambridge, MA: Harvard Business Review Press.

Gren, L., Torkar, R. and Feldt, R. (2017) Group development and group maturity when building agile teams: A qualitative and quantitative investigation at eight large companies, *Journal of Systems and Software*, 124: 104–119.

Grobman, G.M. (2005) Complexity theory: A new way to look at organizational change, *Public Administration Quarterly*, 29 (3): 351–384.

Gryphon, S., Kruchten, P. and McConnell, S. (2006) Letters: The Cone of Uncertainty, *IEEE Software*, 23 (5): 8–10.

Hardingham, A. (1998) *Psychology for Trainers*. London: CIPD.

Hawkins, P. (2017) *Leadership Team Coaching: Developing Collective Transformational Leadership*, 3rd edition. London: Kogan Page.

HBR Ideacast (2019a) Improve your critical thinking at work, *Harvard Business Review*, podcast. Available at: https://hbr.org/podcast/2019/07/improve-your-critical-thinking-at-work (accessed 23 March 2020).

HBR Ideacast (2019b) Why 'connector' managers build better talent, *Harvard Business Review*, podcast. Available at: https://hbr.org/podcast/2019/11/why-connector-managers-build-better-talent (accessed 27 January 2020).

HBR Ideacast (2019c) How companies like Google and Alibaba respond to fast-moving markets, *Harvard Business Review*, podcast. Available at: https://hbr.org/podcast/2019/10/how-companies-like-google-and-alibaba-respond-to-fast-moving-markets (accessed 6 March 2020).

HBR Ideacast (2019d) How one CEO successfully led a digital transformation, *Harvard Business Review*, podcast. Available at: https://hbr.org/podcast/2019/12/how-one-ceo-successfully-led-a-digital-transformation (accessed 20 February 2020).

HBR Webcast (2019) Leading transformation to the intelligent enterprise, *Harvard Business Review*, webcast. Available at: https://hbr.org/webinar/2019/10/leading-transformation-to-the-intelligent-enterprise (accessed 11 February 2021).

Highsmith, J. (2001) History: The Agile Manifesto. Available at: http://agilemanifesto.org (accessed 10 October 2019).

IDEO Futures (2016) Jake Knapp + John Zeratsky from GV, *podtail*, 11 February. Available at: https://podtail.com/en/podcast/ideo-futures/episode-29-jake-knapp-john-zeratsky-from-gv-extend/ (accessed 28 July 2020).

InfoQ (2019) Mastering remote meetings, *eMag*, issue 78, October. Available at: https://www.infoq.com/minibooks/remote-meetings/ (accessed 11 February 2021).

Ingrassia, L. (2020) They changed the way you buy your basics, *The New York Times*, 23 January. Available at: https://www.nytimes.com/2020/01/23/business/Billion-Dollar-Brands.html (accessed 25 January 2020).

Jackson, P.Z. (2003) *58 ½ Ways to Improvise in Training*. Bancyfelin: Crown House.

Johnson, W. (2020) Leading remotely, *MIT Sloan Management Review*, 31 October. Available at: https://sloanreview.mit.edu/article/leading-remotely/ (accessed 29 July 2020).

Joiner, B. and Josephs, S. (2007) *Leadership Agility: Five Levels of Mastery for Anticipating and Initiating Change*, Kindle edition. San Francisco, CA: Jossey-Bass.

Kahneman, D. (2011) *Thinking Fast and Slow*, Kindle edition. London: Penguin.

Katzenbach, J. and Smith, D. (1993) *The Wisdom of Teams*, Kindle edition. Boston, MA: McKinsey.

Kim, G., Behr, K. and Spafford, G. (2013) *The Phoenix Project*. Portland, OR: IT Revolution.

Kim, G., Humble, J., Debois, P. and Willis, J. (2016) *The DevOps Handbook*, Kindle edition. Portland, OR: IT Revolution Press.

Kline, N. (1999) *Time to Think: Listening to Ignite the Human Mind*, Kindle edition. London: Octopus Books.

Knapp, J. and Zeratsky, J. (2016) *Sprint: How to Solve Big Problems and Test New Ideas in Just Five Days*, Kindle edition. London: Transworld.

Larman, C. (2004) *Agile and Iterative Development: A Manager's Guide*. London: Addison-Wesley.

Larman, C. and Vodde, B. (2009) *Lean Primer*, Version 1.6. Available at: https://www.leanprimer.com/downloads/lean_primer.pdf (accessed 5 May 2020).

Leary-Joyce, J. (2014) *The Fertile Void: Gestalt Coaching at Work*, Kindle edition. St. Albans: AoEC Press.

Leary-Joyce, J. and Lines, H. (2018) *Systemic Team Coaching*. St. Albans: AoEC Press.

Lim, S. (2020) How to get away from work mode during the coronavirus lockdown, *Nature*, 30 June. Available at: https://www.nature.com/articles/d41586-020-01976-4 (accessed 3 August 2020).

Lipmanowicz, H. and McCandless, K. (2013) *The Surprising Power of Liberating Structures: Simple Rules to Unleash a Culture of Innovation*. Seattle, WA: Liberating Structures Press.

Little, T. (2006) Schedule estimation and uncertainty surrounding the cone of uncertainty, *IEEE Software*, 23 (3): 48–54.

Maslow, A. (1943) A theory of human motivation, *Psychological Review*, 50 (4): 370–396.

McFadzean, E. (1999) Creativity in MS/OR: Choosing the appropriate technique, *Interfaces*, 29: 110–122.

McKinsey & Company (2017) *How to Create an Agile Organization*. Available at: https://www.mckinsey.com/business-functions/organization/our-insights/how-to-create-an-agile-organization# (accessed 11 February 2021).

Melo, de O. C., Cruzes, D.S., Kon, F. and Conradi, R. (2013) Interpretative case studies on agile team productivity and management, *Information and Software Technology*, 55 (2): 412–427.

Microsoft (2020) What's new in Microsoft teams | July 2020, *Microsoft Tech Blog*, 31 July. Available at: https://techcommunity.microsoft.com/t5/microsoft-teams-blog/what-s-new-in-microsoft-teams-july-2020/ba-p/1551561 (accessed 6 August 2020).

Misra, S.C., Kumar, V. and Kumar, U. (2009) Identifying some important success factors in adopting agile software development practices, *Journal of Systems and Software*, 82 (11): 1869–1890.

Moe, N.B., Dingsøyr, T. and Dybå, T. (2010) A teamwork model for understanding an agile team: A case study of a Scrum project, *Information and Software Technology*, 52: 480–491.

Nonaka, I. and Takeuchi, H. (1996) The knowledge creating company: How Japanese companies create the dynamics of innovation, *Organization*, 3: 303–310.

Ohno, T. ([1978] 1988) *Toyota Production System: Beyond Large-scale Production*. Boca Raton, FL: CRC Press.

Olson, E. and Eoyang, G. (2001) *Facilitating Organization Change: Lessons from Complexity Science*, Kindle edition. San Francisco, CA: Jossey-Bass/Pfeiffer.

Palmer, S. and Whybrow, A., eds. (2007) *Handbook of Coaching Psychology: A Guide for Practitioners*. Hove: Taylor & Francis.

Pascale, R. (1990) *Managing on the Edge*. London: Penguin.

Passmore, J. (2007) Behavioural coaching, in S. Palmer and A. Whybrow (eds.) *Handbook of Coaching Psychology: A Guide for Practitioners*. Hove: Routledge.

Pemberton, C. (2015) *Resilience: A Practical Guide for Coaches*, Kindle edition. Maidenhead: Open University Press.

Pichler, R. (n.d.) *The Product Vision Board*. Available at: https://www.romanpichler.com/tools/product-vision-board/ (accessed 17 June 2020).

Poppendieck, M. and Poppendieck, T. (2007) *Implementing Lean Software Development: From Concept to Cash*, Kindle edition. Boston, MA: Addison-Wesley.

Poppendieck, M. and Poppendieck, T. (2014) *The Lean Mindset: Ask the Right Questions*, Kindle edition. Upper Saddle River, NJ: Addison-Wesley.

Renjen, P. (2019) The 4 types of leader who will thrive in the Fourth Industrial Revolution, *World Economic Forum*. Available at: https://www.weforum.org/agenda/2019/01/these-four-leadership-styles-are-key-to-success-in-the-fourth-industrial-revolution/ (accessed 6 March 2020).

Re Turner, L. (2018) *Succeeding with Agile: What Makes Agile Transformations Successful?* Dissertation for the MSc in Coaching and Behavioural Change, Henley Business School, Henley-on-Thames.

Re Turner, L. (2020) Here's how to create engaging learning experiences online, *Medium*, 20 April. Available at: https://medium.com/icagile/tips-from-an-experienced-icagile-online-course-facilitator-fd7cfc46bb0d.

Ries, E. (2011) *The Lean Startup: How Relentless Change Creates Radically Successful Businesses*, Kindle edition. London: Penguin.

Rigby, D., Sutherland, J. and Takeuchi, H. (2016) Embracing Agile: How to master the process that's transforming management, *Harvard Business Review*, May. Available at: https://hbr.org/2016/05/embracing-agile (accessed 11 February 2021).

Rigby, D., Sutherland J. and Noble, A. (2018) Agile at scale, *Harvard Business Review*, May/June. Available at: https://hbr.org/2018/05/agile-at-scale (accessed 11 February 2021).

Rogers, C. ([1961] 2004) *On Becoming a Person: A Therapist's View of Psychotherapy*. London: Constable.

Rogers, J. (2010) *Facilitating Groups*. Maidenhead: Open University Press.

Schein, E. (2009) *The Corporate Culture Survival Guide*, Kindle edition. San Francisco, CA: Wiley.

Schwab, K. (2016) The Fourth Industrial Revolution: What it means, how to respond, *World Economic Forum*, 14 January. Available at: https://www.weforum.org/agenda/2016/01/the-fourth-industrial-revolution-what-it-means-and-how-to-respond/ (accessed 25 May 2020).

Schwaber, K. (2011) *The Path to Agility 2010: Ken Schwaber pt1*, YouTube: ThePathTo-Agility. Available at: https://www.youtube.com/watch?v=BGhJnLLBWpA (accessed 1 May 2018).

Schwaber, K. and Sutherland, J. (2017) *The Scrum Guide. The Definitive Guide to Scrum: The Rules of the Game.* Available at: https://scrumguides.org/scrum-guide.html (accessed 30 November 2019).

Senge, P. (1993) Transforming the practice of management, *Human Resource Development Quarterly*, 4: 5–32.

Senge, P. (2006) *The Fifth Discipline: The Art & Practice of the Learning Organisation.* London: Random House.

Senge, P. (2010) *The Fifth Discipline Fieldbook: Strategies and Tools for Building a Learning Organization*, Kindle edition. London: Nicholas Brealey.

Singer-Velush, N., Sherman, K. and Anderson, E. (2020) Microsoft analyzed data on its newly remote workforce, *Harvard Business Review*, 15 July. Available at: https://hbr.org/2020/07/microsoft-analyzed-data-on-its-newly-remote-workforce (accessed 10 August 2020).

Somers, M. (2020) How a collaborative spirit feeds innovation at an IDEA design lab, *Ideas Made to Matter*, MIT Management Sloan School, 8 April. Available at: https://mitsloan.mit.edu/ideas-made-to-matter/how-a-collaborative-spirit-feeds-innovation-ikea-design-lab (accessed 28 March 2020)

Spayd, M.K. and Adkins, L. (2011) *Developing Great Agile Coaches: Towards a Framework of Agile Coaching Competency – Part 1.* Boulder, CO: Agile Coaching Institute.

Stacey, R.D. (1995) The science of complexity: An alternative perspective for strategic change processes, *Strategic Management Journal*, 16 (6): 477–495.

Stacey, R.D. (1996) Emerging strategies for a chaotic environment, *Long Range Planning*, 29 (2): 182–189.

Stacey, R.D. (2000) The emergence of knowledge in organizations, *Emergence*, 2 (4): 23–39.

Sutherland, J. and Schwaber, K. (2007) *The Scrum Papers: Nuts, Bolts and Origins of an Agile Process.* Available at: http://citeseerx.ist.psu.edu/viewdoc/download?doi=10.1.1.108.814&rep=rep1&type=pdf (accessed 4 April 2018).

Takeuchi, H. and Nonaka, I. (1986) The new new product development game, *Harvard Business Review*, January. Available at: https://hbr.org/1986/01/the-new-new-product-development-game (accessed 11 February 2021).

Taylor, B. (2017) How Coca-Cola, Netflix, and Amazon learn from failure, *Harvard Business Review*, 10 November. Available at: https://hbr.org/2017/11/how-coca-cola-netflix-and-amazon-learn-from-failure (accessed 11 February 2021).

Tes (2020a) How we work, *Musings of the Tes Engineering Team*. Available at: https://engineering.tes.com/how-we-work/ (accessed 11 February 2021).

Tes (2020b) Remote First in Tes Technology, *Musings of the Tes Engineering Team*. Available at: https://engineering.tes.com/remote-first/ (accessed 11 February 2021).

The Open University (2020) Mastering systems thinking in practice, *OpenLearn*, The Open University. Available at: https://www.open.edu/openlearn/science-maths-technology/mastering-systems-thinking-practice/content-section-overview (accessed 28 May 2020).

Thomas, B. (2019) 3 priorities for CEOs in 2019, *World Economic Forum*. Available at: https://www.weforum.org/agenda/2019/01/ceo-priorities-for-success-in-2019/ (accessed 24 March 2020).

Turner, E. (2020) *Be Less Zombie*, Kindle edition. New York: Wiley.

Verheyen, G. (2013) *Scrum: A Pocket Guide*, Kindle edition. Zaltbommel: Van Haren Publishing.

Walsh, D. (2020) 3 practices for effective work in a remote world, *Ideas Made to Matter*, MIT Management Sloan School, 13 July. Available at: https://mitsloan.mit.edu/ideas-made-to-matter/3-practices-effective-work-a-remote-world (accessed 11 February 2021).

Waterman, R.H., Jr., Peters, T.J. and Phillips, J.R. (1980) Structure is not organization, *Business Horizons*, 23v (3): 14–26. Available at: https://managementmodellensite.nl/webcontent/uploads/Structure-is-not-organization.pdf (accessed 11 February 2021).

Whittington, J. (2016) *Systemic Coaching & Constellations*, 2nd edn, Kindle edition. London: Kogan Page.

Wikipedia (2020a) *Humanistic psychology*. Available at: https://en.wikipedia.org/wiki/Humanistic_psychology (accessed 11 February 2021).

Wikipedia (2020b) *Action learning*. Available at: https://en.m.wikipedia.org/wiki/Action_learning (accessed 21 August 2020).

Williams, L. (2012) What Agile teams think of Agile principles, *Communications of the ACM*, 55 (4): 71–76.

Woudstra, G. (2020) *The Art of Team Coaching*, recording, 13 February. Lichfield: ICF UK. Available at: https://www.coachfederation.org.uk/events/detail/webinar-recording/the-art-of-team-coaching (accessed 11 February 2021).

# Index